HMH Florida Science

Grade 2

This Write-In Book belongs to

____

Teacher/Room

____

The zebra longwing is the state butterfly of Florida. These insects feed on plant nectar and pollen.

Houghton Mifflin Harcourt

Consulting Authors

Michael A. DiSpezio
Global Educator
North Falmouth, Massachusetts

Marjorie Frank
Science Writer and Content-Area Reading Specialist
Brooklyn, New York

Michael R. Heithaus, Ph.D.
Dean, College of Arts, Sciences & Education
Professor, Department of Biological Sciences
Florida International University
Miami, Florida

Cover: ©Flame/Alamy

Florida Standards courtesy of the Florida Department of Education.

Printed in the U.S.A.

ISBN 978-1-328-79357-7

4 5 6 7 8 9 10 0868 26 25 24 23 22 21 20 19 18
4500709168 BCDEFG

Contents

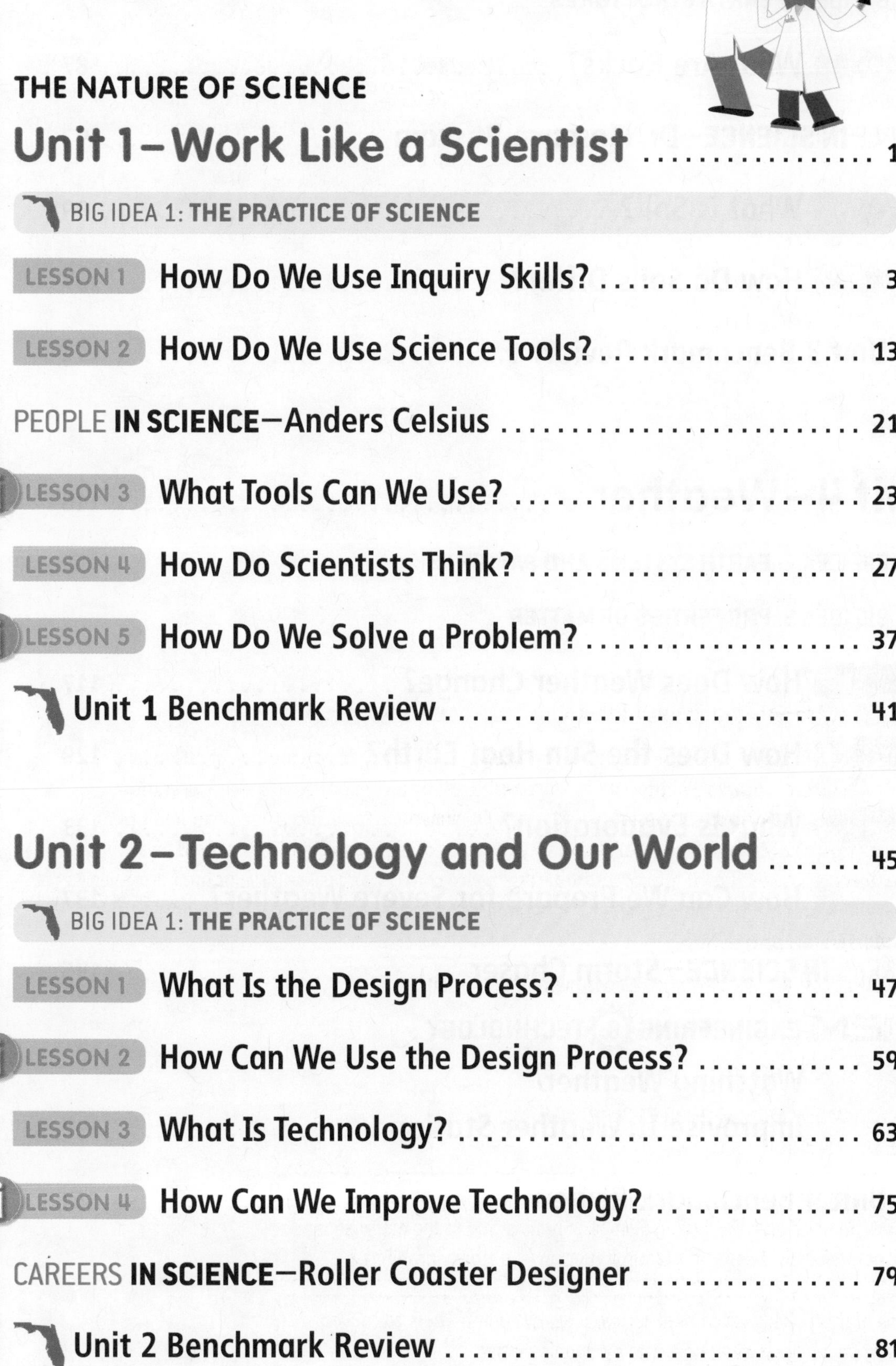

EARTH AND SPACE SCIENCE

Unit 3 – Earth's Surface 85

Unit 4 – Weather 115

PHYSICAL SCIENCE

Unit 5—All About Matter

Unit 6—Matter Can Change

PHYSICAL SCIENCE

Unit 7—Energy

Unit 8—Forces and Motion

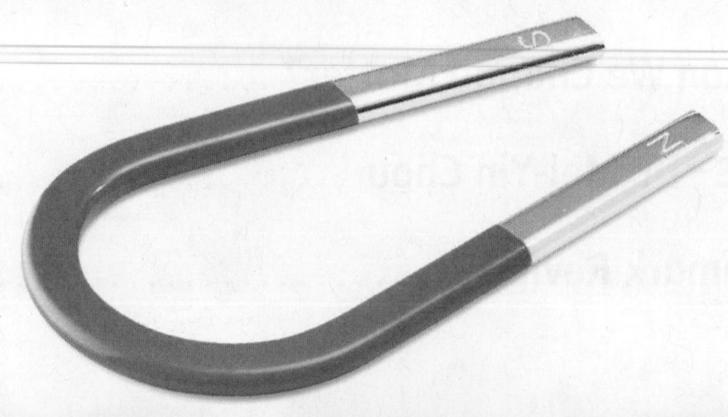

LIFE SCIENCE

Unit 9 – The Human Body

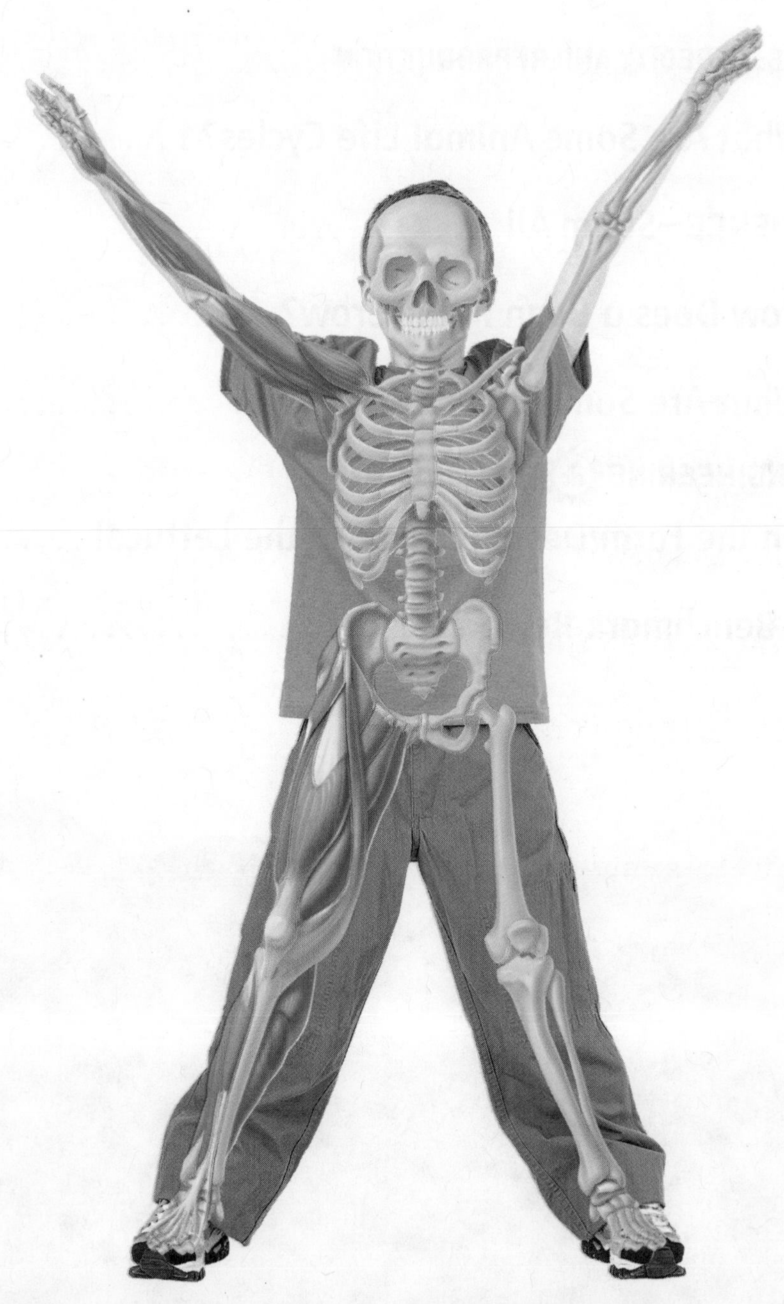

LIFE SCIENCE

Unit 10 – Life Cycles

LIFE SCIENCE

Unit 11 – Basic Needs and Environments

21st Century Skills: Technology and Coding

Safety in Science

Here are some safety rules to follow when you do activities.

1. Think ahead.
   Study the steps and follow them.

2. Be neat and clean.
   Wipe up spills right away.

3. Watch your eyes.
   Wear safety goggles when told to do so.

4. Be careful with sharp things.

5. Do not eat or drink things.

Work Like a Scientist

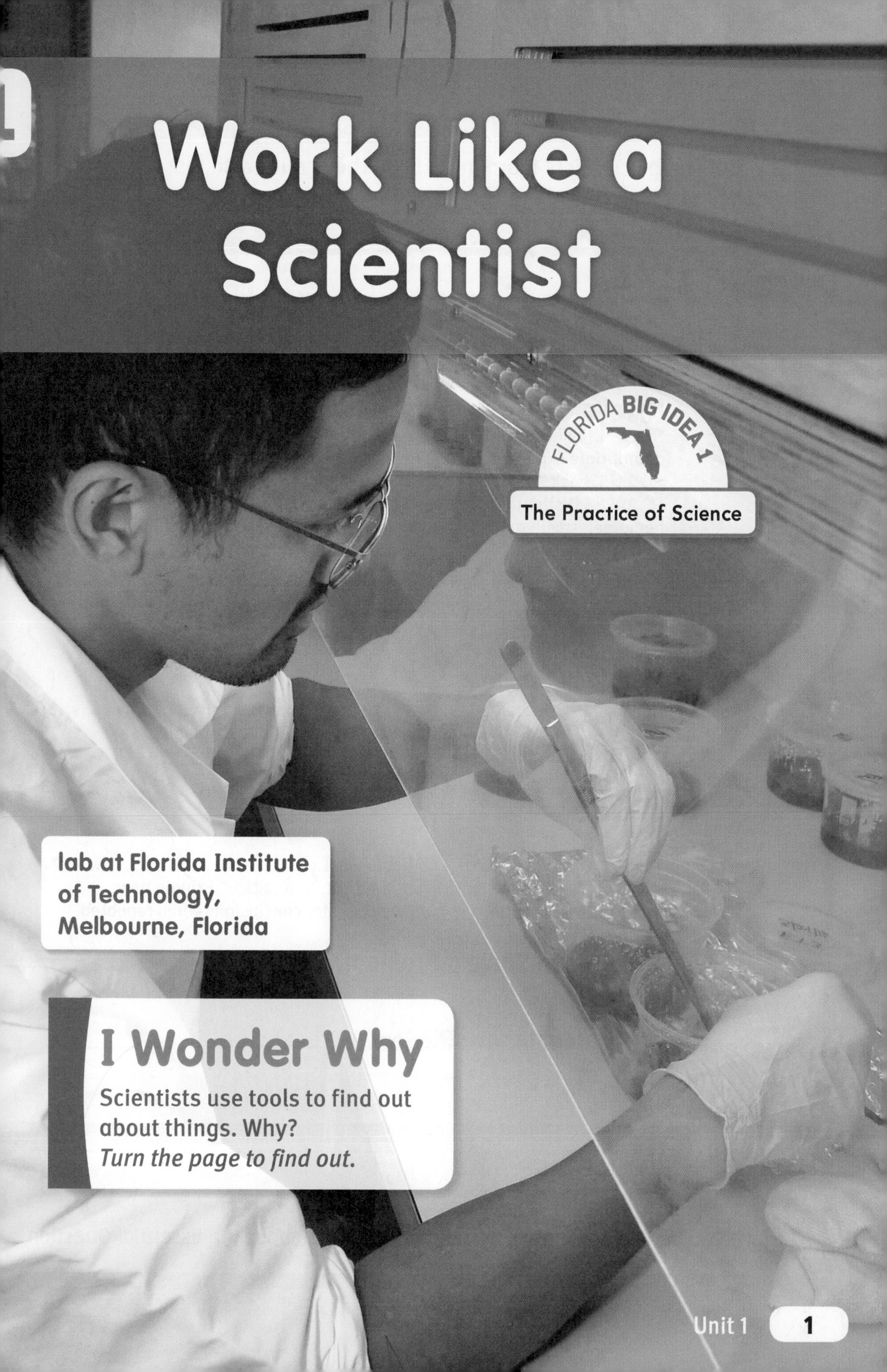

FLORIDA BIG IDEA 1

The Practice of Science

lab at Florida Institute of Technology, Melbourne, Florida

I Wonder Why

Scientists use tools to find out about things. Why?
Turn the page to find out.

Here's Why

Tools help scientists learn more than they could with just their senses.

Essential Questions and Florida Benchmarks

Science Notebook

Before you begin each lesson, write your thoughts about the Essential Question.

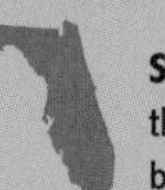

SC.2.N.1.1 Raise questions . . . investigate them in teams . . . and generate appropriate explanations based on those explorations. **SC.2.N.1.3** Ask "how do you know?" in appropriate situations . . . **SC.2.N.1.5** Distinguish between empirical observation . . . and ideas or inferences . . .

LESSON 1

Essential Question

How Do We Use Inquiry Skills?

Engage Your Brain

Find the answer in this lesson.

You tell how these flowers are alike and different.

You are ________ them.

Active Reading

Lesson Vocabulary

1 Preview the lesson.

2 Write the vocabulary term here.

____

Use Inquiry Skills

Inquiry skills help people find out information. Inquiry skills help people plan and do tests.

These children use inquiry skills to do a task for school. They are observing. Observe means to use your five senses to learn about things.

Active Reading

Find the sentence that tells the meaning of **observe**. Draw a line under the sentence.

Danny and Sophie want to observe things in the backyard. They plan an investigation. They plan how to find out what they want to know. They also predict, or make a good guess, about what they will observe.

▶ **This page names three inquiry skills. Circle the name for one of the skills.**

Explore the Backyard

Danny and Sophie head out to the backyard to begin their task. Danny finds the length and the height of the birdhouse. He measures it with a ruler.

Active Reading

Find the sentence that explains what it means to **measure**. Draw a line under the sentence.

They use inquiry skills to learn more about the backyard.

Sophie compares leaves. She observes how they are alike and how they are different. She may also classify, or sort, many leaves in the backyard by the way they are alike.

▶ **Look at Sophie's leaves. Put them in order of size from smallest to largest.**

2 ______ 1 ______ 3 ______

Model and Infer

Now Danny and Sophie draw a map of the backyard. They are making a model to show what something is like. You could also make a model to show how something works.

Active Reading

Find the sentences that explain what it means to **make a model**. Draw a line under the sentences.

Danny and Sophie use one more inquiry skill. They **infer**. They use what they know to answer a question—Are there any living things in the backyard? They can infer that the backyard is home to many plants and animals.

▶ **Think about what you know about winter. Infer what Danny and Sophie might observe in the backyard during winter.**

____

____

Sum It Up »

1 Complete It!

Fill in the blank.

How are measuring, observing, and predicting alike?

They are all

_____________________.

2 Circle It!

Circle the skill name to match the meaning.

Which one means to choose steps you will do to learn something?

infer

plan an investigation

classify

3 Draw and Write It!

Observe something outside. Then draw and write to record your observations.

____

____

Brain Check

Name ____________________

Vocabulary Review

Read each clue below. Then unscramble the letters to write the correct answer.

observe **compare** **measure** **infer**

1. to find the size or amount of something

   s e m a r e u measuhe

2. to use your senses to learn about something

   b o s r e e v obsrve

3. to observe how things are alike and different

   p o c r a m e compare

4. to use what you know to answer a question

   f n i r e infer

Apply Concepts

Match each inquiry skill to its meaning.

to make a good guess about what will happen	plan an investigation
to sort things by how they are alike	classify
to show what something is like or how it works	predict
to follow steps to answer a question	make a model

Family Members: See ***ScienceSaurus®*** for more information about observations and investigations.

SC.2.N.1.2 Compare the observations made by different groups using the same tools.

LESSON 2

Essential Question

How Do We Use Science Tools?

Engage Your Brain

Find the answer to the question in the lesson.

What does a thermometer measure?

____

Active Reading

Lesson Vocabulary

1. Preview the lesson.
2. Write the 2 vocabulary terms here.

________________ ________________

Top Tools

You use tools every day. Tools are things that help you do a job. **Science tools** help you find out information.

A hand lens is one science tool. It helps you observe more details than with your eyes alone.

A hand lens makes things look larger.

Measuring Tools

You use some tools for measuring things. You use a **thermometer** to measure temperature. You use a measuring cup to measure amounts of liquids.

Active Reading

The main idea is the most important idea about something. Draw a line under the main idea on this page.

A thermometer measures temperature in units called degrees.

A measuring cup measures liquids in units called milliliters, cups, or ounces.

Measure More!

You use a tool called a scale to measure weight. You can use a balance to measure mass.

This scale measures weight in units called pounds and ounces.

▶ **Name two things you can weigh on a scale.**

____

____

This balance measures mass in units called grams and kilograms.

You use a ruler and a tape measure to measure distance as well as length, width, and height. Both tools measure in units called inches or centimeters.

▶ Circle the object the ruler is measuring.

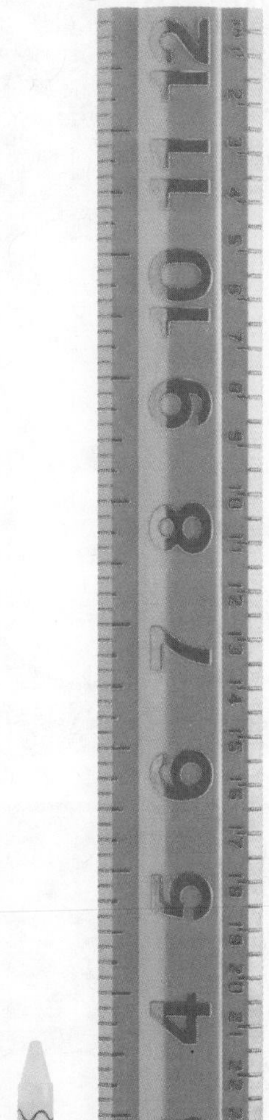

A ruler measures objects with straight lines.

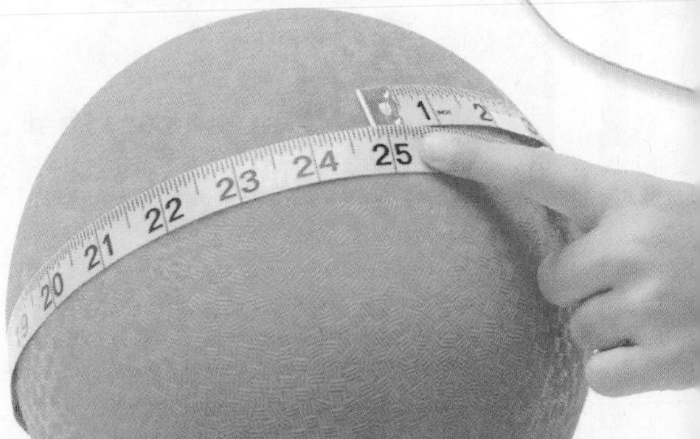

A tape measure can measure around an object.

Sum It Up »

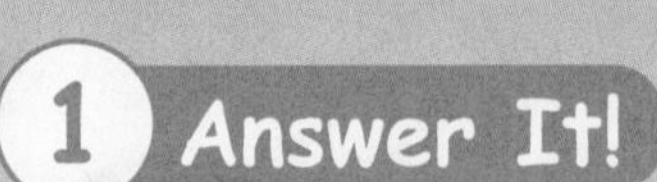

Write the answer to this question.

You want to measure how much water fits into a pail. What tool could you use?

____

2 Draw It!

Draw yourself using a measuring tool.

Mark an X on the tool that does not measure.

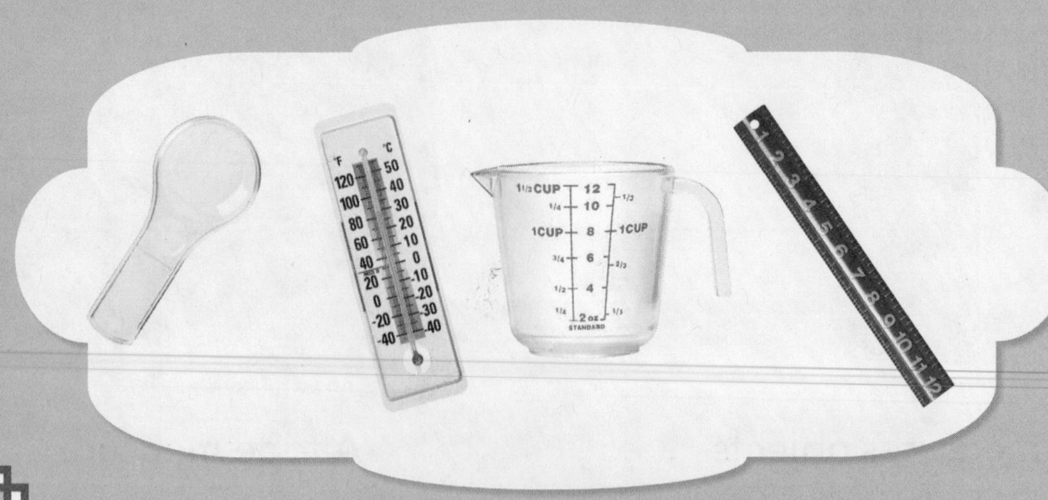

Brain Check

Name ____________________

Vocabulary Review

Match the name of each tool to its picture.

tape measure	
balance	
thermometer	
measuring cup	
hand lens	

Apply Concepts

Name the tool you could use for each job.

measuring the length of a book	ruler
finding the weight of a watermelon	scab
observing curves and lines on the tip of your finger	hand lens

Family Members: Go on a scavenger hunt. See which tools from this lesson you have in or around your home. Discuss with your child how to use each tool.

SC.2.N.1.2 Compare the observations made by different groups using the same tools. SC.2.N.1.6 Explain how scientists alone or in groups are always investigating new ways to solve problems.

4 Things to Know About Anders Celsius

1

In 1742, Celsius invented the Celsius scale to measure temperature.

2

The temperature at which water freezes on the Celsius scale is 0°.

3

The temperature at which water boils on the Celsius scale is 100°.

4

Celsius was an astronomer, or a person who studies the stars and other things in space.

Celsius Match Up

1

°C 50 40 30 20 10 0 -10 -20

▶ Read each thermometer. Write the number that matches the correct temperature in each picture.

2

3

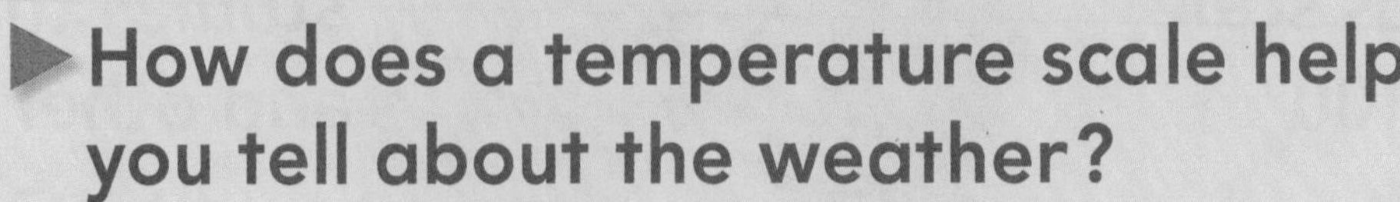

▶ How does a temperature scale help you tell about the weather?

____

____

____

SC.2.N.1.1 Raise questions about the natural world, investigate them in teams through free exploration and systematic observations, and generate appropriate explanations based on those explorations. SC.2.N.1.2 Compare the observations made by different groups using the same tools.

Name ________________________________

Essential Question

What Tools Can We Use?

Materials

box of objects

box of science tools

EXPLORE

How do science tools help you learn about things? Investigate to find out.

Before You Begin—Preview the Steps

1. Choose an object from the box. Record what you observe about the object.
2. Choose a tool. Use it to observe your object.
3. What more does the tool help you learn about the object? Record what you learn.
4. Compare your observations with those of classmates.

Set a Purpose

Write what you want to find out.

Think About the Procedure

1. Which science tool did you choose? What does it do?

2. How will the tool help you observe the object?

Name ______________________

Record Your Data

Draw and write to record your observations.

My Object ______________________

My Tool ______________________

What I Learned Without the Tool	What I Learned With the Tool

Claims • Evidence • Reasoning

1. Write a claim about how a science tool can help you learn more about an object.

2. What evidence supports your claim?

3. Why does your evidence support your claim?

Ask More Questions

What other questions can you ask about how science tools are used?

SC.2.N.1.1 Raise questions . . . investigate them . . . and generate appropriate explanations based on those explorations. SC.2.N.1.3 Ask "how do you know?" in appropriate situations . . . SC.2.N.1.4 Explain how . . . scientific investigations should yield similar conclusions . . . SC.2.N.1.5 Distinguish between empirical observation . . . and ideas or inferences . . .

LESSON 4

Essential Question

How Do Scientists Think?

Engage Your Brain

Find the answer in the lesson.

When scientists

____

they follow steps and use tools to answer a question.

Active Reading

Lesson Vocabulary

1 Preview the lesson.

2 Write the 4 vocabulary terms here.

________________ ________________

________________ ________________

Let's Observe It

Scientists **investigate**. They plan and do a test to answer a question or solve a problem. They use inquiry skills and science tools to help them.

There are many ways to investigate. But many scientists follow a sequence, or order of events. Here's one possible sequence. First, scientists may observe and ask a question.

Active Reading

Clue words can help you find the orc of things. **First** is a clue word. Circle this clue word in the paragraph abo

▶ What objects will these children use for their test? Circle them.

Now, scientists can make hypothesis. A **hypothesis** is statement that can be tested. hen scientists plan a fair test. he scientists list the materials ey will need and the steps they ill take to do their test.

Let's Test It!

Next, the scientists are ready to do their test. They follow their plan and record what they observe.

Active Reading

Clue words can help you find the order of things. **Next** is a clue word. Circle this clue word in the paragraph above.

These children test whether food coloring spreads faster in cold water or warm water.

After the test, scientists **draw conclusions**. They use the information they have gathered to decide if their results support the hypothesis. Finally, they write or draw to **communicate** what they learned.

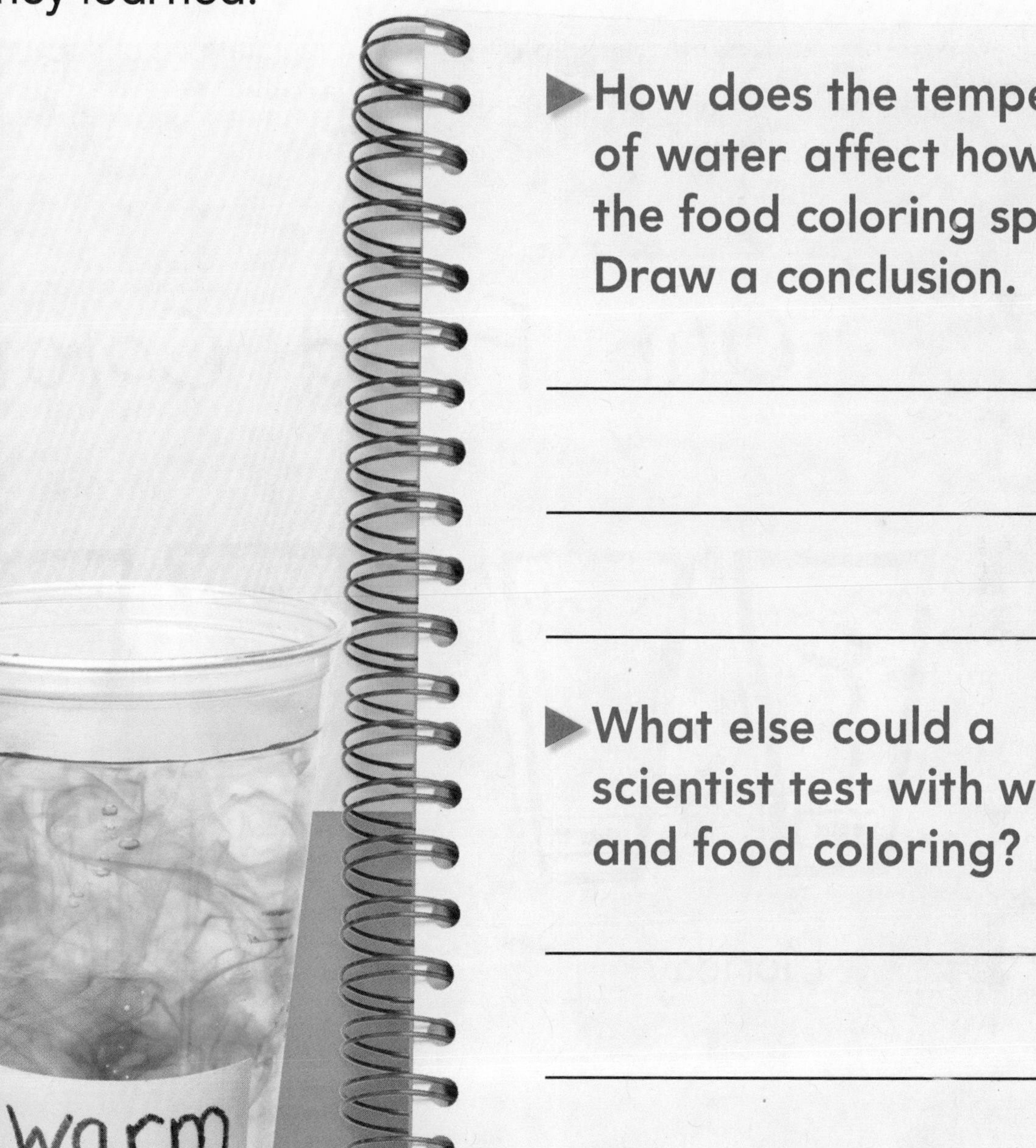

▶ **How does the temperature of water affect how fast the food coloring spreads? Draw a conclusion.**

___

___

___

▶ **What else could a scientist test with water and food coloring?**

___

___

___

Let's Check Again

Scientists do the same test a few times. They need to make sure that they get similar results every time. In this investigation, the food coloring should spread faster in warm water every time.

ook at the warm cup for both Monday and Friday. Draw a conclusion. Color in the warm cup for Wednesday to show what it should look like.

Measure Temperature

Choose an object. Use a ruler to measure the object's length. Measure it three times. Record.

Length of ________	
Measure 1	
Measure 2	
Measure 3	

1. How do your numbers compare?

____

____

2. Why do you think so?

____

____

____

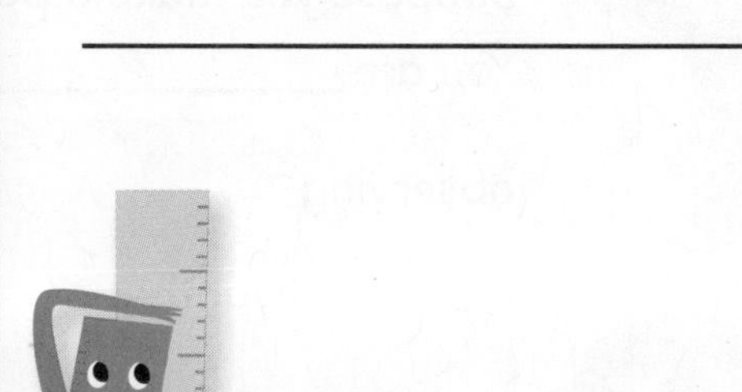

Sum It Up »

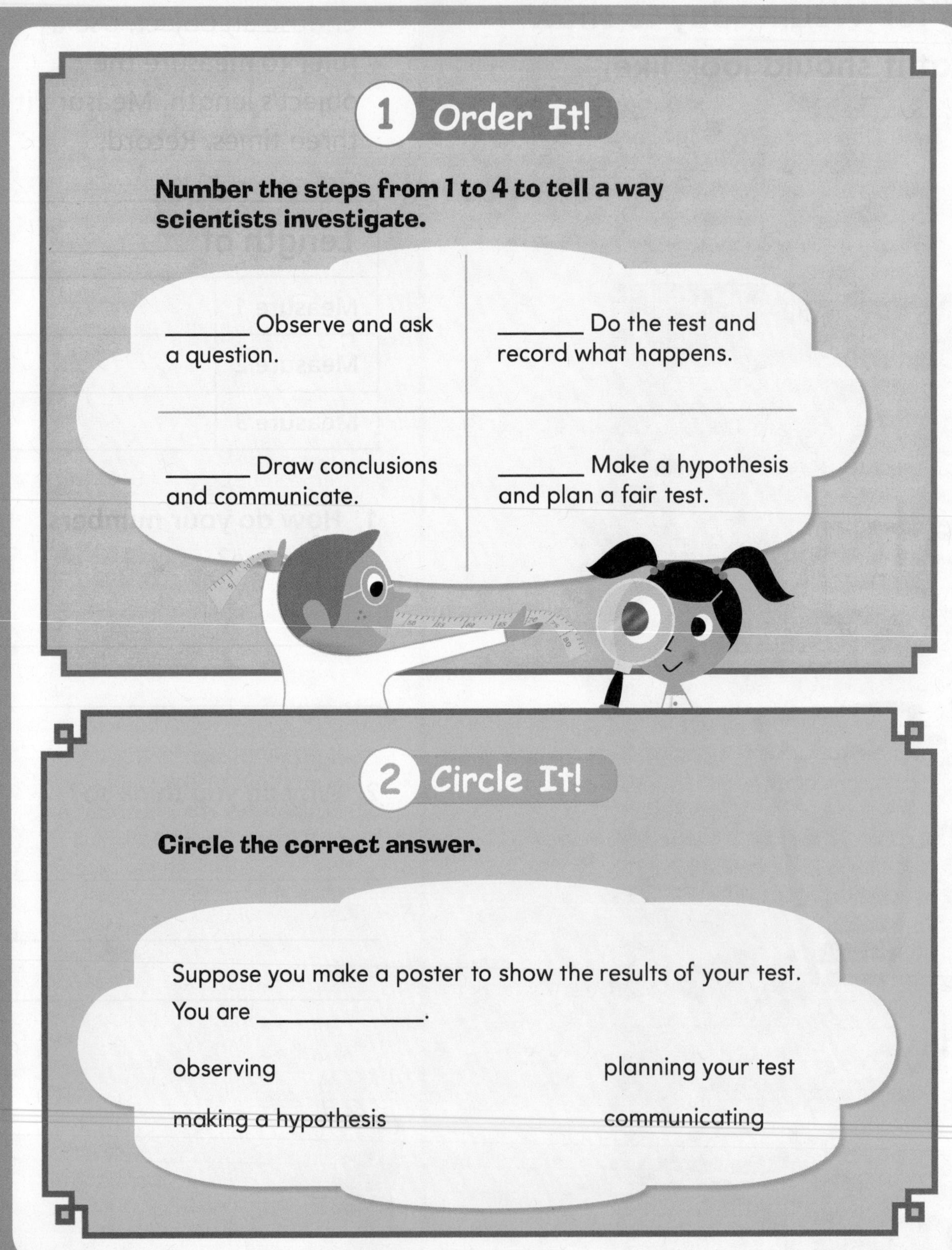

1 Order It!

Number the steps from 1 to 4 to tell a way scientists investigate.

_______ Observe and ask a question.

_______ Do the test and record what happens.

_______ Draw conclusions and communicate.

_______ Make a hypothesis and plan a fair test.

2 Circle It!

Circle the correct answer.

Suppose you make a poster to show the results of your test. You are _____________.

observing

planning your test

making a hypothesis

communicating

Brain Check

Name ______________________

Vocabulary Review

Circle the word to complete each sentence.

1. You use inquiry skills and science tools to learn.
   You ____________.

   communicate investigate

2. You take the first step to do an investigation.
   You ____________.

   draw conclusions observe

3. You make a statement that you can test.
   You make a ____________.

   hypothesis conclusion

4. You use information you gathered to explain what you learned. You ____________.

   draw conclusions observe

5. You write to tell about the results of a test.
   You ____________.

   communicate ask a question

Apply Concepts

These steps show a test some children did. Label each box with a step from this lesson.

The children look at an ice cube. They ask—
Will it melt in the sun?
Observe and ________________.

↓

They form a statement that the ice cube will melt in the sun.
________________.

↓

They follow their plan. The ice cube melts! They decide that the sun's heat caused the ice to melt.
Test and ________________.

↓

The children write and draw to tell the results of their test.
________________.

Family Members: Work with your child to plan an investigation. Use the steps from this lesson.

SC.2.N.1.1 Raise questions about the natural world, investigate them in teams through free exploration and systematic observations, and generate appropriate explanations based on those explorations. SC.2.N.1.6 Explain how scientists alone or in groups are always investigating new ways to solve problems.

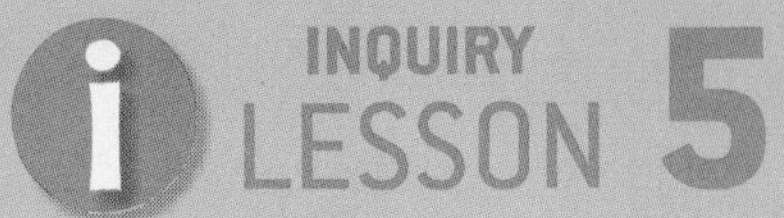

Name ________________________________

Essential Question

How Do We Solve a Problem?

EXPLORE

You want to organize art supplies in your classroom. Design and build a holder to keep them organized.

Materials

- scissors
- glue
- tape
- string
- cardboard
- construction paper
- cans
- cartons

Before You Begin—Preview the Steps

1. List the properties the holder must have. For example, the holder must be strong enough to hold the weight of the supplies.
2. Use your list to design your holder. Make a drawing. Think of materials you could use.
3. Build your holder.
4. Test your holder. Improve it.

Set a Purpose

What will you do?

____

____

____

Think About the Procedure

1. Why do you make a list of the properties the holder must have?

____

____

____

2. Why do you design your holder before you build it?

____

____

Name ______________________

Record Your Data

Write the details of your plan in this chart.
Draw your model.

The Problem
My Plan
Materials I Need
My Model

Claims • Evidence • Reasoning

1. Write a claim about how your solution worked.

2. What evidence supports your claim?

3. Why does your evidence support your claim?

4. How could you redesign your organizer to make it better?

Ask More Questions

What other questions do you have about designing and making models to solve problems?

UNIT 1
Benchmark Review

Name ______________________

Vocabulary Review

Use the terms in the box to complete the sentences.

communicate
investigate
thermometer

1. When you draw or write, you communicate.

2. A tool that measures temperature is a(n) thermometer.

3. When you plan and do a test to answer a question, you investigate.

Science Concepts

Fill in the letter of the choice that best answers the question.

4. Sumeet looks at the sky before he goes to school. It is dark and cloudy outside. What skill is Sumeet using?
   - Ⓐ comparing
   - Ⓑ inferring
   - Ⓒ observing

5. Victor weighs a melon. It weighs 3 pounds. Ana measures the same melon. What should Ana observe?
   - Ⓐ The melon weighs 2 pounds.
   - Ⓑ The melon weighs 3 pounds.
   - Ⓒ The melon weighs 4 pounds.

6. Reem uses this tool to find the length of a book.

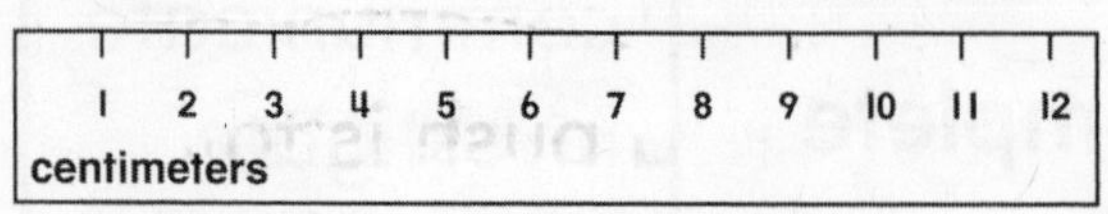

What is she doing?

Ⓐ classifying
Ⓑ inferring
Ⓒ measuring

7. Jia wants to find out how the temperature in the afternoon compares to the morning temperature. What should she do?

Ⓐ Infer the afternoon temperature. Then compare it to the morning temperature.
Ⓑ Measure the afternoon temperature. Then compare it to the morning temperature.
Ⓒ Predict the afternoon temperature. Then compare it to the morning temperature.

8. Lea investigates the answer to a question. Then she repeats her experiment. Which will **most likely** be true?

Ⓐ The results will be the same.
Ⓑ The results will be different.
Ⓒ She cannot compare the results.

9. Carlos finishes an investigation. He draws this picture in a notebook.

Why does Carlos draw the picture?

Ⓐ to plan the investigation
Ⓑ to predict what will happen
Ⓒ to record what he observed

Name ______________________

10. Jared knows that his two blocks are the same color but different shapes. How does he know?

Ⓐ He measures them.
Ⓑ He makes a model.
Ⓒ He observes and compares them.

11. You think that an ant and a butterfly have the same parts. Why would models help you find out if this is true?

Ⓐ The models would be the same size as the real insects.
Ⓑ The models would show parts that the real insects have.
Ⓒ Making models would mean that you do not have to make observations.

12. Kate makes a claim that science tools can help her learn whether a tree or a bush is taller. Which tool can she use to find evidence to support her claim?

Ⓐ
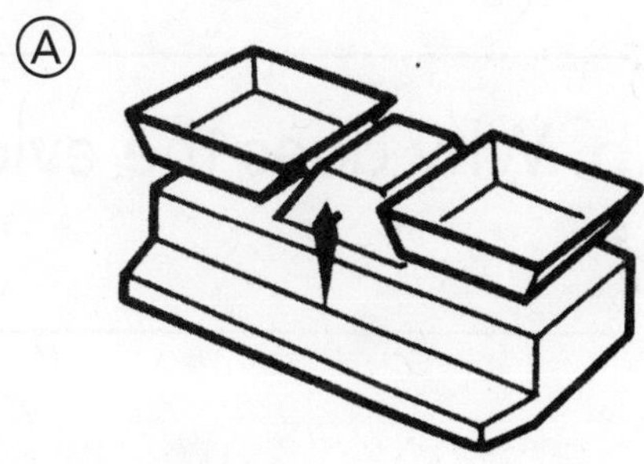

Ⓑ
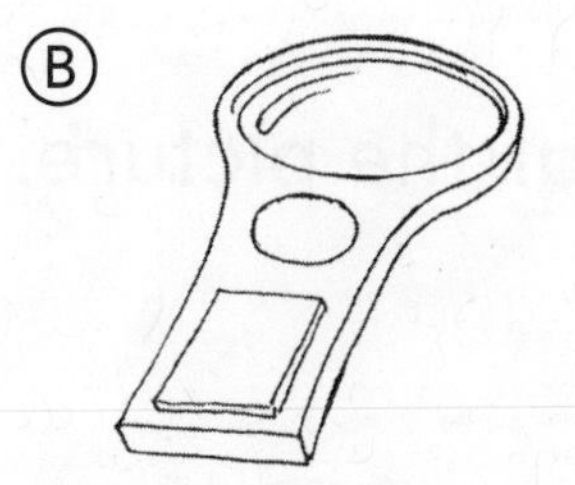

Ⓒ
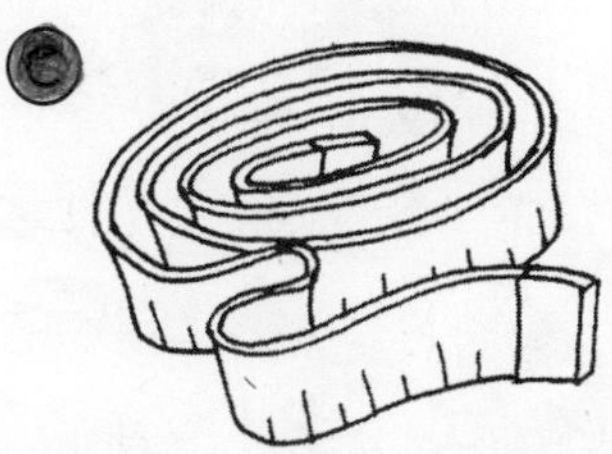

Inquiry and the Big Idea

Write the answers to these questions.

13. Pete designs a paper airplane that should fly 15 feet. He makes the claim that his design works.

   a. What evidence would support his claim?

   ____

   b. Why does the evidence support the claim?

   ____

   ____

14. Look at the picture.

   a. What science tool is the boy using?

   ____

   b. What is he doing?

   ____

2

Technology and Our World

FLORIDA BIG IDEA 1

The Practice of Science

The Dali Museum,
St. Petersburg, Florida

I Wonder How

An engineer planned a design for these buildings. How?
Turn the page to find out.

Here's How

An engineer drew a plan for the buildings. The plan showed these interesting shapes.

Essential Questions and Florida Benchmarks

Science Notebook

Before you begin each lesson, write your thoughts about the Essential Question.

SC.2.N.1.1 Raise questions ... investigate them in teams ... and generate appropriate explanations based on those explorations. **SC.2.N.1.3** Ask "how do you know?" in appropriate situations ... **SC.2.N.1.6** Explain how scientists ... solve problems.

Essential Question

What Is the Design Process?

Engage Your Brain

Find the answer to the question in the lesson.

How could you keep the dog leashes from getting tangled?

You could ________

________.

Active Reading

Lesson Vocabulary

1. Preview the lesson.
2. Write the 2 vocabulary terms here.

________ ________

Get Real!

Look at the engineers at work! **Engineers** solve problems by using math and science. The answers they find help people.

Engineers work in many areas. Some engineers design cars. Some make robots. Others find ways to make the world cleaner or safer.

Active Reading

Find the sentence that tells the meaning of **engineers**. Draw a line under that sentence.

A civil engineer plans bridges and roads.

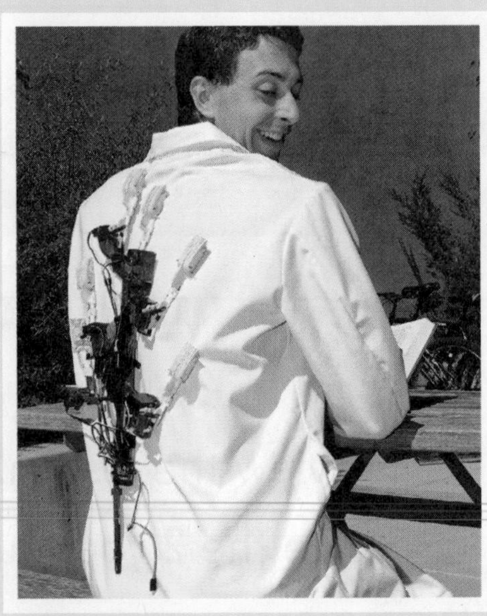

A robotics engineer designs robots.

The Design Process

How do engineers solve a problem? They use a design process. A **design process** is a set of steps that engineers follow to solve problems.

This engineer checks on a building project.

An aerospace engineer may work on airplanes or rockets.

▶ Circle the names of three kinds of engineers.

A Tangled Mess!

When Kate walks her dogs, their leashes always get tangled. She needs to solve this problem. How can a design process help?

1 Find a Problem

Kate's first step is to name her problem. What is wrong? What does she want to do? Then Kate brainstorms ways to solve her problem.

Active Reading

Things may happen in order. Write 1 next to what happens first. Write 2 next to what happens next.

Kate gets out her Science Notebook. She will keep good records. She will show how she plans and builds the solution to her problem.

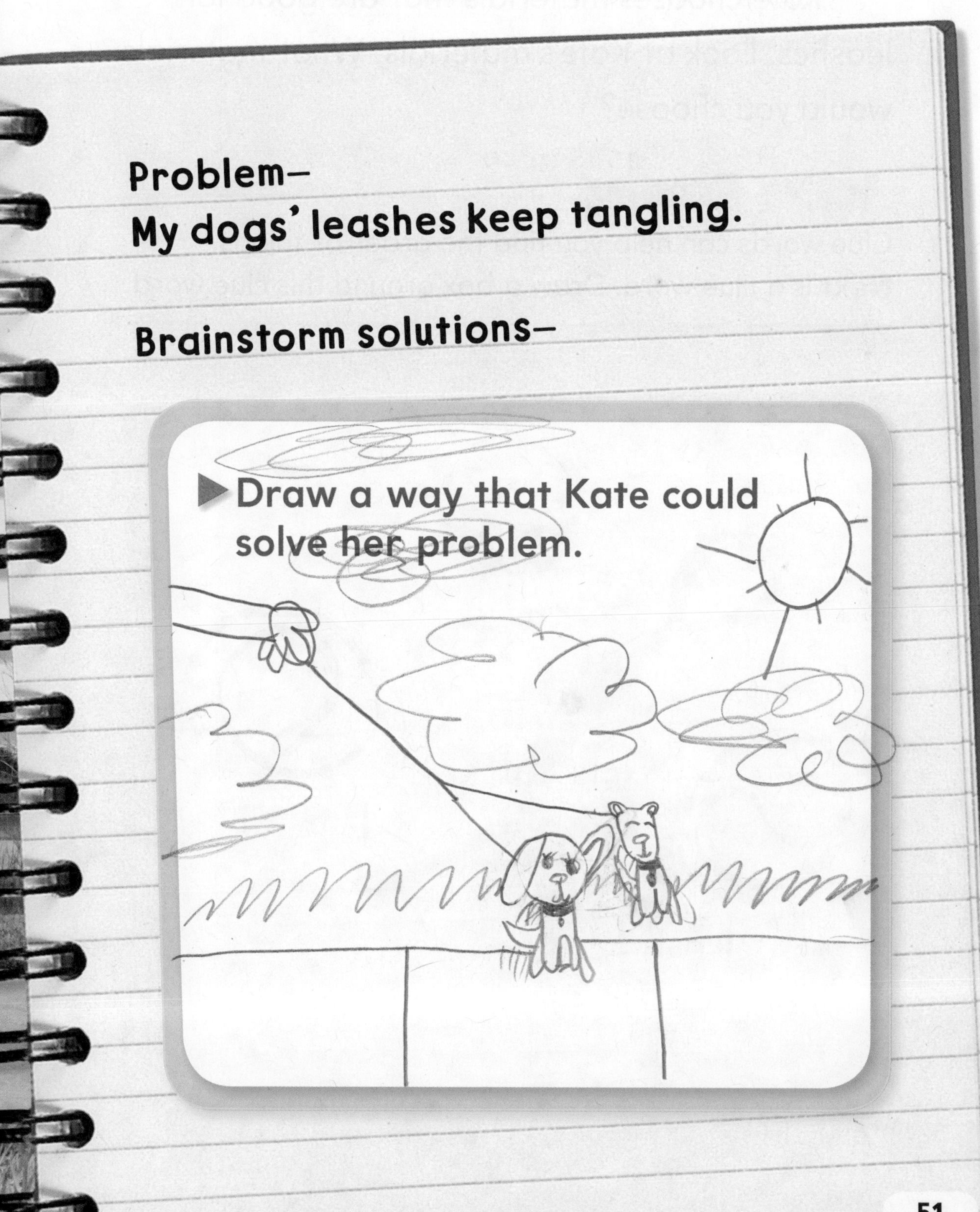

2 Plan and Build

Next, Kate chooses a solution to try. She makes a plan. She draws and labels her plan.

Kate chooses materials that are good for leashes. Look at Kate's materials. What materials would you choose?

Active Reading

Clue words can help you find the order of things. **Next** is a clue word. Draw a box around this clue word.

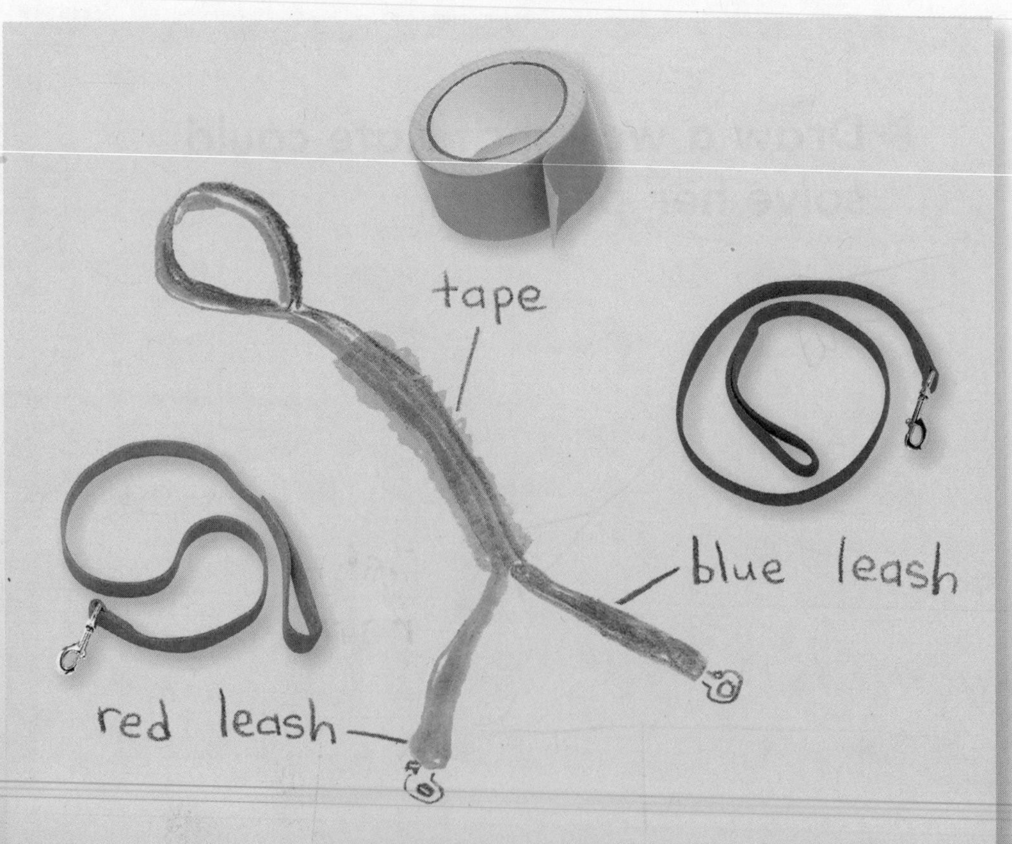

Kate follows her plan to make her new leash.
The new leash may be the solution to her problem!

▶ **How does planning help Kate build her new leash?**

____

____

3 Test and Improve

It is time for Kate to find out whether the new leash works. She tests it when she walks the dogs. Kate will know the leash works if it does not tangle.

4 Redesign

Kate thinks of ways to improve her new leash. She writes notes about how to make her design better.

5 Communicate

Kate shows the results of her test. She takes a picture of her design. She also writes about what happened during the test.

Ways to make the design better—make the leash parts or the handle longer.

My Results—

1. Red and blue parts of the new leash did not tangle.
2. My feet bumped the dogs as I walked.

▶ Circle the part of the results that tells about a problem with the leash.

Sum It Up »

1 Circle It!

Circle the step of the design process shown here.

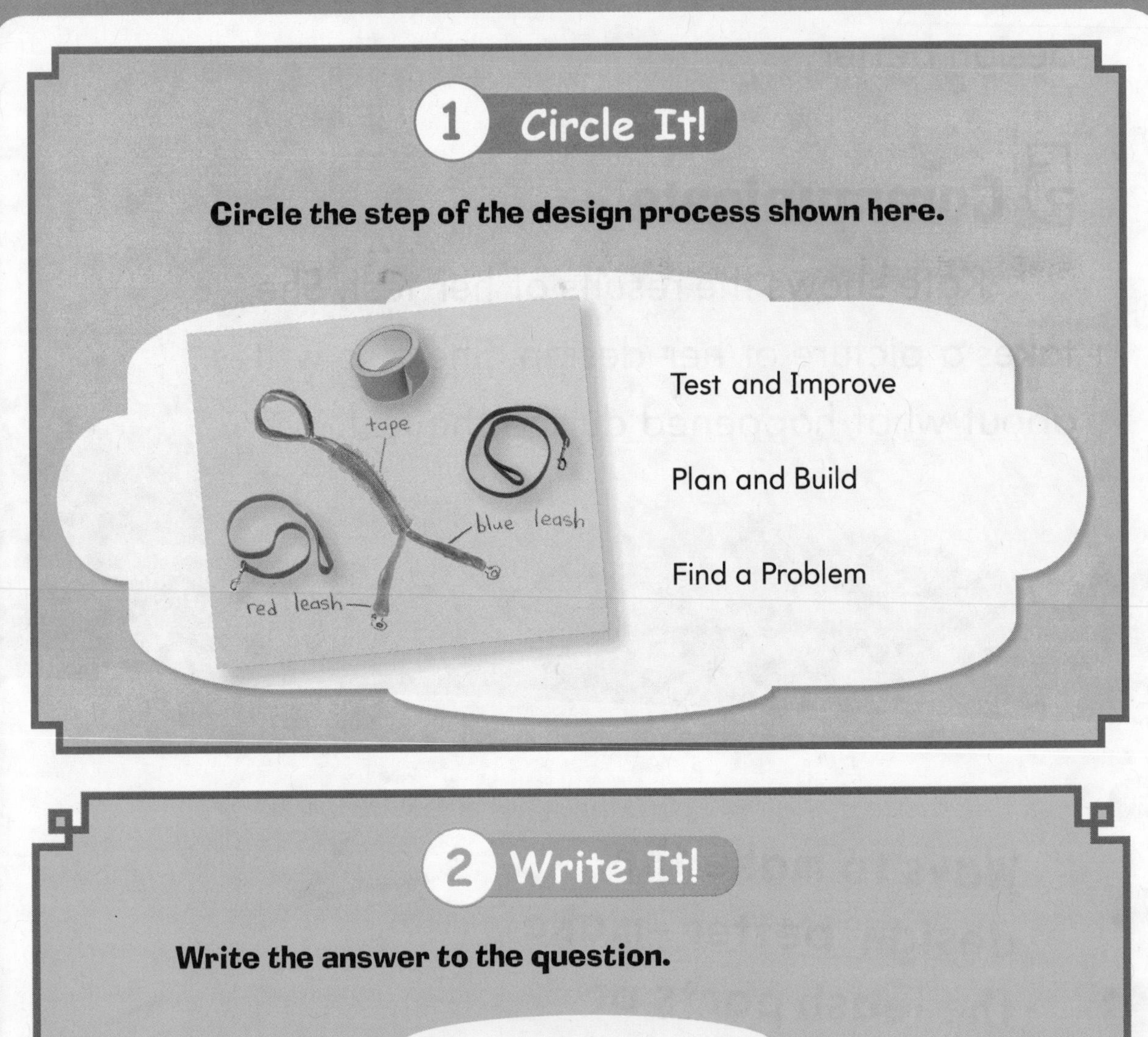

Test and Improve

Plan and Build

Find a Problem

2 Write It!

Write the answer to the question.

Why is it important to keep good records?

____

____

____

Brain Check

Name ______________________

Vocabulary Review

Match the terms in the box with each clue.

design process materials solution test

steps that engineers follow to solve a problem

d e s i g n p r o c e s s
(1 under d, 3 under g, 2 under n)

the answer to a problem

s o l u t i o n
(4 under i, 5 under n)

how you find out whether a solution works

t e s t
(6 under e)

things you use to make a design

m a t e r i e l e
(7 under e, 8 under r)

Solve the riddle. Write the numbered letters in order on the lines below.

I am a scientist who uses math and science to solve problems. Who am I?

E n g i n e e r
1 2 3 4 5 6 7 8

Apply Concepts

Complete the flowchart with the steps of the design process.

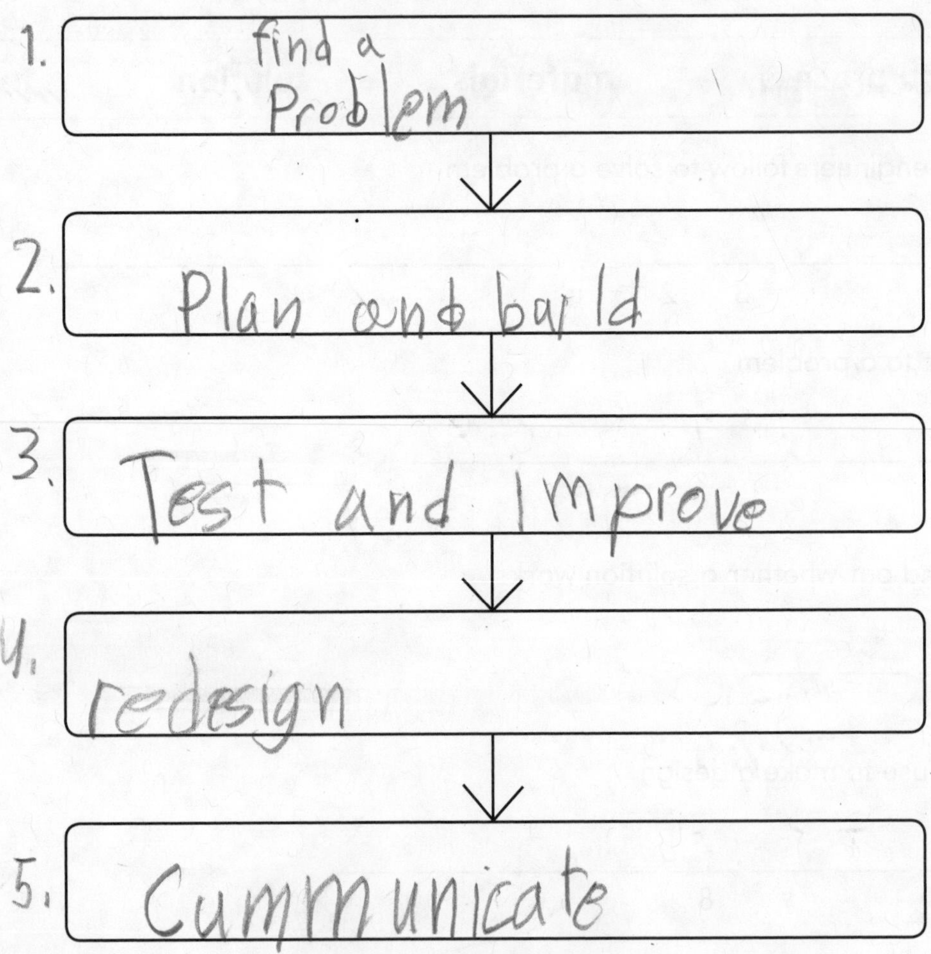

Family Members: See *ScienceSaurus*® for more information about engineers and technology.

SC.2.N.1.1 Raise questions ..., investigate them in teams ..., and generate appropriate explanations based on those explorations. SC.2.N.1.3 Ask "how do you know?" in appropriate situations ... SC.2.N.1.6 Explain how scientists...solve problems.

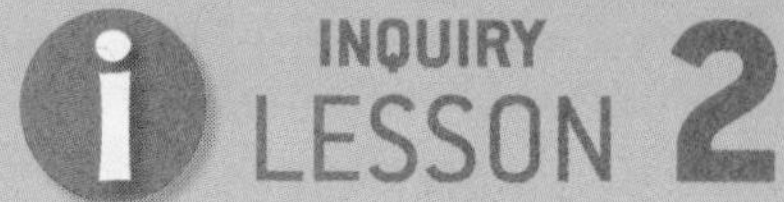

Name ___________________________

Essential Question

How Can We Use the Design Process?

Material

classroom materials

EXPLORE

Your best pencil keeps falling to the bottom of your backpack. What can you design to make your pencil easier to find?

Before You Begin—Preview the Steps

1. Plan your solution. Then follow your plan to build your solution. Be sure to keep good records.
2. Test and improve your solution.
3. Redesign your solution.
4. Communicate the results.

Set a Purpose

What will you do?

____

____

____

Think About the Procedure

1. Why do you need to plan your solution?

____

____

____

2. Why do you need to test your solution?

____

____

Name ______________________

Record Your Data

1. Draw to communicate your solution and the test results. Label the materials. Write a caption to tell how your solution works.

2. Draw and label the redesign of your solution.

Claims • Evidence • Reasoning

1. Write a claim about how the design process helped you solve the problem.

2. What evidence supports your claim?

3. Why does evidence support your claim?

Ask More Questions

What other questions could you ask about using the design process?

Essential Question

What Is Technology?

Engage Your Brain

Find the answer to the question in the lesson.

You use the technology in this picture every day.

What is it?

It is a

________________________.

Active Reading

Lesson Vocabulary

1. Preview the lesson.
2. Write the 2 vocabulary terms here.

________________ ________________

By Design

Did you use a toothbrush or turn on a light today? Both a toothbrush and a light are kinds of technology. **Technology** is what engineers make to meet needs and solve problems. Anything people design to help us do things is technology.

Find the sentence that tells the meaning of technology. Draw a line under the sentence.

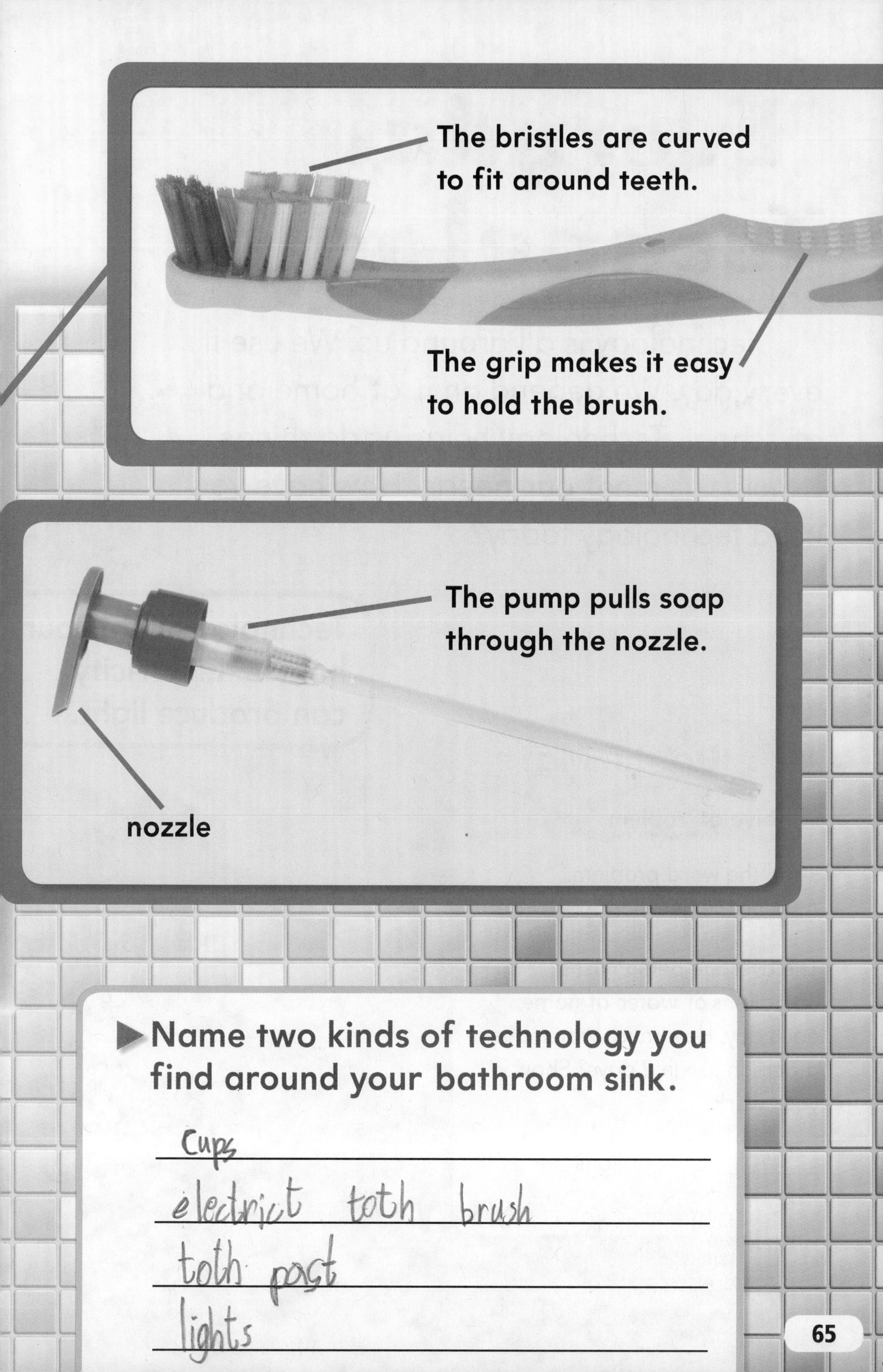

▶ Name two kinds of technology you find around your bathroom sink.

Cups
electrict toth brush
toth past
lights

Everyday Technology

Technology is all around us. We use it every day. We depend on it at home and at school. Technology helps us do things. It helps us meet our needs. How have you used technology today?

Technology lights our homes. Electricity can produce light.

Do the Math

Solve a Problem

Read the word problem. Answer the question.

The average person uses 80 gallons of water at home each day. How much water does a person use in 2 days? Show your work.

______________ gallons

When the power goes out, so do electric lights. What other technology could you use to light your home?
light a candle.
antern.
Technology helps bring clean water to our homes.
Technology helps us make food. An oven, stovetop, and microwave oven cook food and heat water.

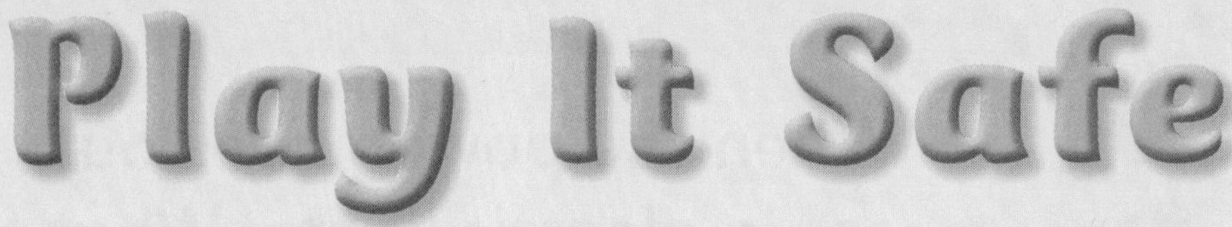

Play It Safe

Technology can be helpful when we use it with care. It can be unsafe if we do not use it with care.

We should use each kind of technology the way it was designed to be used. We should wear safety gear if we need to. Using technology correctly helps us stay safe.

Active Reading

The main idea is the most important idea about something. Draw two lines under the main idea.

The things that keep us safe are technology, too!

▶ What technology keeps you safe in a car?

____

____

____

Environmental Effects

Technology can affect the environment. An **environment** is all the living and nonliving things in a place.

Batteries, for example, are a helpful technology. They provide power to phones, cars, toys, and other things. But they can harm the environment, too.

When old batteries break down, they can pollute water and soil.

Some batteries can be used over and over again. Most batteries can be recycled. How do you think this helps the environment?

▶ Write two ways you can keep batteries from being thrown away.

____

____

____

Sum It Up »

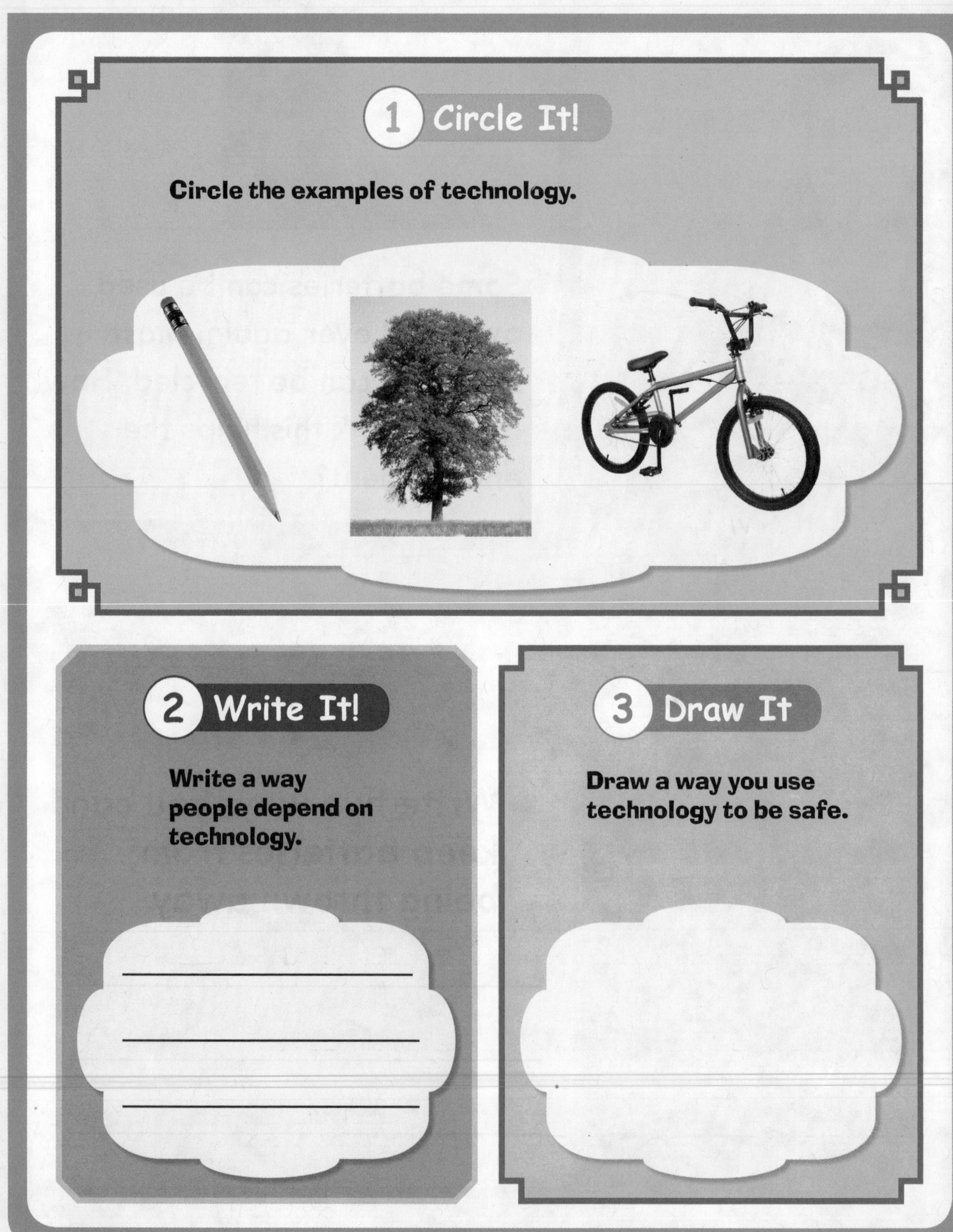

1 Circle It!
Circle the examples of technology.
2 Write It!
Write a way people depend on technology.
3 Draw It
Draw a way you use technology to be safe.

Brain Check

Name ______________________

Vocabulary Review

Match each word to its meaning.

what engineers make to meet needs and solve problems	environment
all the living and nonliving things in a place	technology

Write two ways technology can affect the environment.

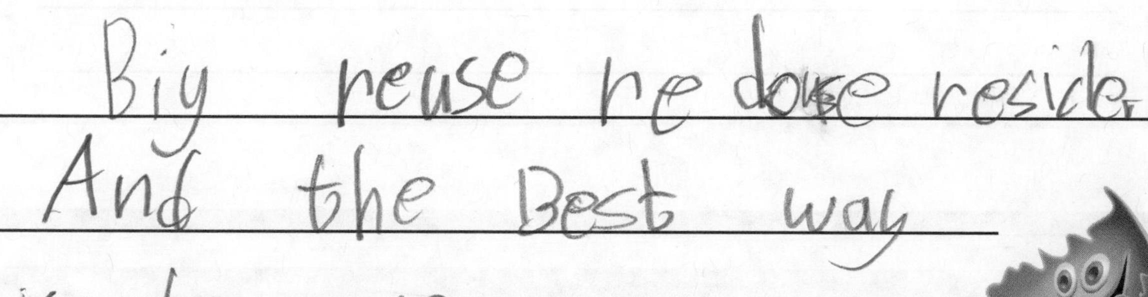

Apply Concepts

Fill in the chart. Write different kinds of technology.

Technology

Technology I Use Every Day
____
____

Technology I Must Use With Care
____
____

Technology That Affects the Environment
____
____

Family Members: Ask your child to point out examples of technology in your home. Discuss how to use the technology safely.

SC.2.N.1.1 Raise questions..., investigate them in teams..., and generate appropriate explanations based on those explorations. SC.2.N.1.3 Ask "how do you know?" in appropriate situations...

INQUIRY LESSON 4

Name ______________________________

Essential Question

How Can We Improve Technology?

Materials

everyday object or tool

craft materials

EXPLORE

How can you improve the things you use everyday? Investigate to find out.

Before You Begin—Preview the Steps

1. Choose an everyday object or tool. Think of ways to make the object work better.
2. Test your ideas.
3. Show your best idea. Draw a picture. Then make a model.

Set a Purpose

Tell what you want to find out.

Think About the Procedure

1. What are some objects you could choose?

2. How could you improve your object?

Name ______________________________

Record Your Data

1. Draw to communicate your solution. Label your picture.

Claims • Evidence • Reasoning

1. Write a claim about how your solution improved the object you chose.

2. What evidence supports your claim?

3. Why does your evidence support your claim?

Ask More Questions

What other questions could you ask about improving technology?

Ask a Roller Coaster Designer

What do roller coaster designers do?
We design roller coasters for amusement parks. We think up ideas for new rides. We also figure out how much they will cost to build.

Do designers work alone?
We work as a team with engineers to make a design. The design has to work and be safe and fun for riders. A factory then builds the ride.

How long does it take to build a roller coaster?
It usually takes about a year from design to finish. A simpler design takes less time.

Now It's Your Turn!

▶ What question would you ask a roller coaster designer?

____

____

____

____

Design Your Own Roller Coaster

▶ Draw your own roller coaster in the space below.

▶ Explain your design. Write about how your roller coaster moves.

Earth's Surface

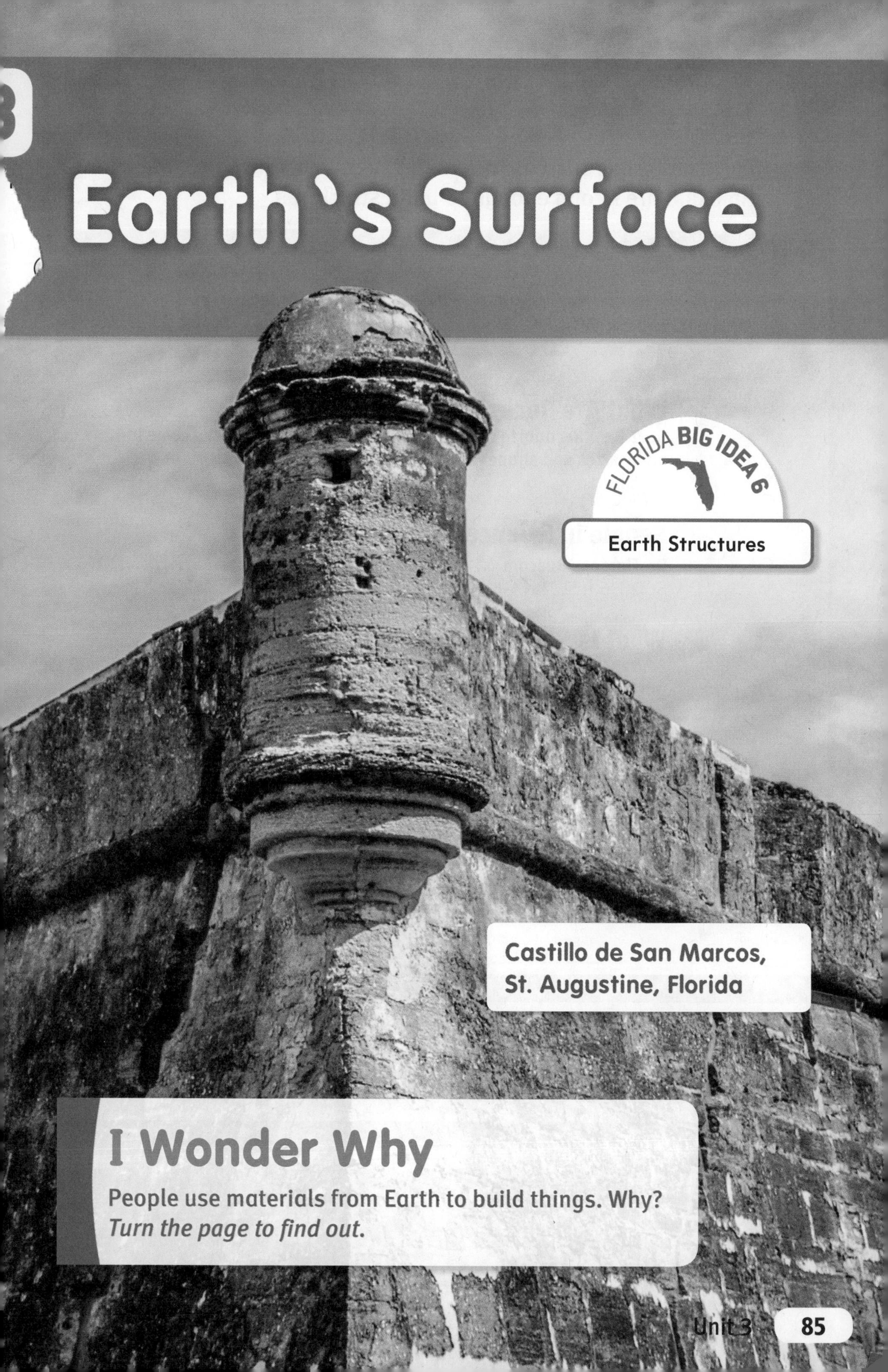

FLORIDA BIG IDEA 6

Earth Structures

Castillo de San Marcos,
St. Augustine, Florida

I Wonder Why

People use materials from Earth to build things. Why?
Turn the page to find out.

Here's Why

Earth materials such as rock are easy to find. They also last a long time and are strong enough to build structures.

Essential Questions and Florida Benchmarks

Science Notebook

Before you begin each lesson, write your thoughts about the Essential Question.

SC.2.E.6.1 Recognize that Earth is made up of rocks. Rocks come in many sizes and shapes.

LESSON 1

ssential Question

What Are Rocks?

Engage Your Brain

Find the answer to the question in the lesson.

Where can you find rocks?

Rocks are all over ____________.

Active Reading

Lesson Vocabulary

1. Preview the lesson.
2. Write the 2 vocabulary terms here.

____________ ____________

Rocks Rock!

Earth is made up of rock. A **rock** is a hard, nonliving object from the ground. Rocks can be different sizes. A boulder is a very large rock. A pebble is a very small rock. Sand is made of many tiny pieces of rock.

boulde

sand

▶ **Name a size of rock you see on this page.**

Weathering changes big rocks into smaller rocks. **Weathering** is what happens when wind and water break down rock into smaller pieces.

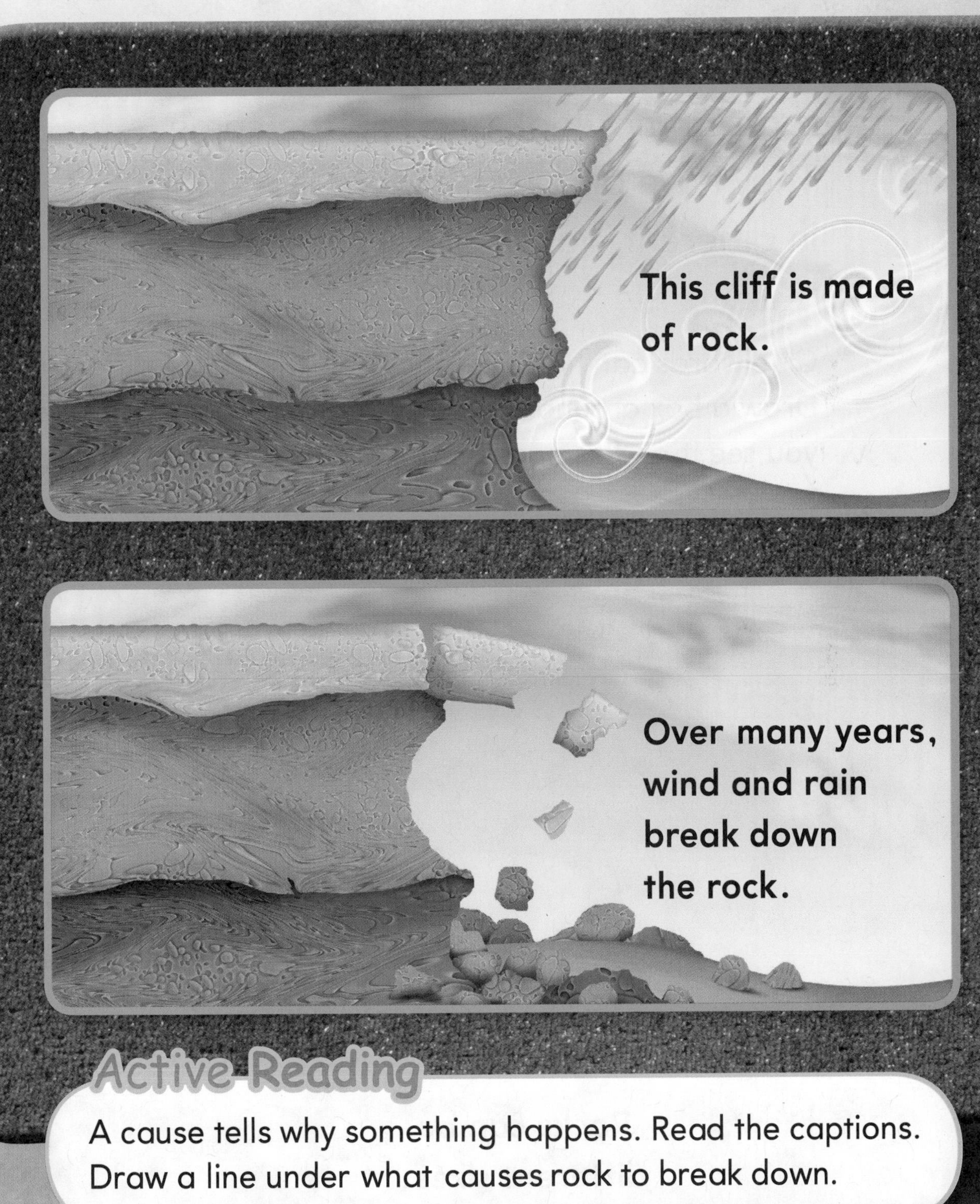

This cliff is made of rock.

Over many years, wind and rain break down the rock.

Active Reading

A cause tells why something happens. Read the captions. Draw a line under what causes rock to break down.

Great Rock Groups

Rocks are made up of minerals. All rocks do not look and feel the same. They have different minerals and form in different ways.

Active Reading

Clue words can help you find ways things are different. Draw a box around the clue word **different** each time you see it on this page.

Size

Rocks can be different sizes.

Shape

Rocks can be different shapes.

▶ Write another way you might group rocks.

____

____

Color

Rocks can be different colors, too.

Rock Resources

People use rocks every day. We use rocks to build things like walls and homes. We use rocks to make art. Rocks are very helpful!

This home and wall are made of rock.

This sculpture is made of rock.

1²3 Do the Math

Solve a Problem

Read the word problem. Answer the questions.

Mike observes a brown rock and a gray rock in his yard. The brown rock weighs 11 pounds. The gray rock weighs 13 pounds.

1. Use > and < to compare the weights of the rocks.

   13 lb. > 11 lb.

   11 lb. < 13 lb.

2. Which rock is heavier?

   the gray rock

Draw one way people use rocks.

Sum It Up »

1 Draw It!

Draw each rock. Then write how the rocks are different.

pebble

very small rock

boulder

very lage rock

2 Write It!

Where can you see rocks around your home? Explain.

. backyard . lake

. Patio . on rode

. bildings.

3 Circle It!

Circle the sentence that is true.

Rocks are made up of minerals.

Rocks have the same shape.

Brain Check

LESSON **1**

Name ______________________

Vocabulary Review

Fill in the blanks. Use each word from the word bank.

rock	pebbles	sand	weathering

The next time you see a big rock, look closely. Someday the rock may be much smaller! Wind and rain may wear away at the rock. This is called weathering. Over time, the rock may break down into small pebbles. Perhaps the pebbles will someday break down into tiny pieces of sand.

Apply Concepts

Fill in the chart. Show how rocks can be alike and different.

Rocks

Alike	Different
made of minerals	size
____________ ____________	____________ ____________
____________ ____________	____________ ____________

Family Members: See ***ScienceSaurus***® for more information about Earth's surfaces.

Learn About...

Dr. Florence Bascom

Dr. Florence Bascom was a geologist, or a person who studies rocks. She began her work in the 1890s. At that time, most women did not study science. Dr. Bascom wanted other women to learn about rocks, so she taught geology at a women's college. She also traveled to the Grand Canyon and other places to study rocks.

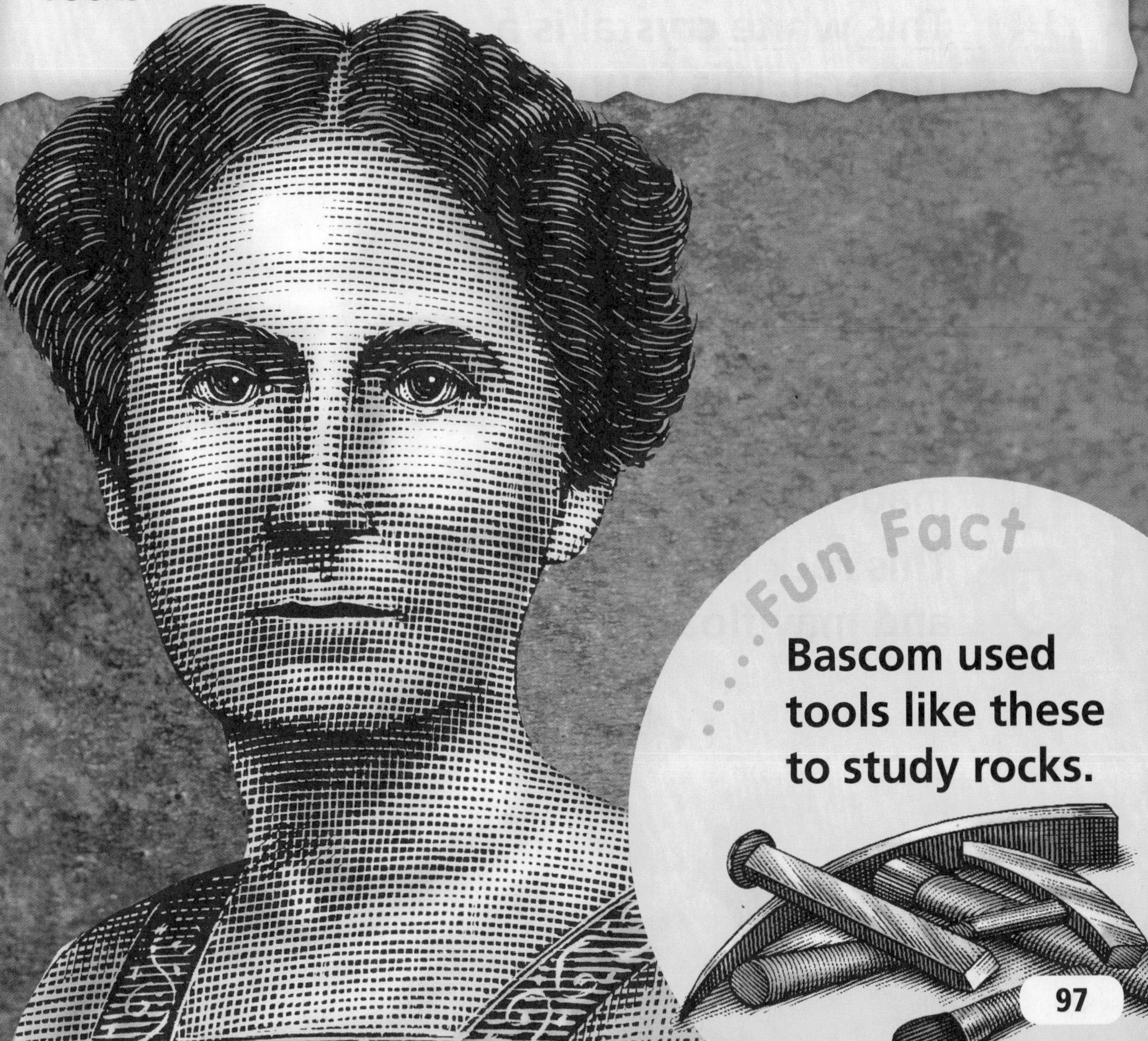

Fun Fact

Bascom used tools like these to study rocks.

Know Your Rocks

Dr. Florence Bascom studied rocks. Here's your chance!

▶ Write the number of each description next to the correct rock.

1. This white rock is used for statues and building materials.
2. This white crystal is a mineral. It is found in many places.
3. This shiny black rock is called volcanic glass. It was formed from lava from a volcano.
4. This brown rock is made of tiny grains.
5. This rock has air holes and may float in water.

2 quartz

4 sandstone

5 pumice

1 marble

3 obsidian

SC.2.E.6.2 Describe how small pieces of rock and dead plant and animal parts can be the basis of soil and explain the process by which soil is formed. SC.2.E.6.3 Classify soil types based on color, texture (size of particles), the ability to retain water, and the ability to support the growth of plants.

LESSON 2

Essential Question

What Is Soil?

Engage Your Brain

Find the answer to the question in the lesson.

How can people use soil?

to ______________

Active Reading

Lesson Vocabulary

1. Preview the lesson.
2. Write the 4 vocabulary terms here.

______________ ______________

______________ ______________

Super Soil

Soil is made up of small pieces of rock and once-living things. We use soil to grow plants.

Active Reading

Find the sentence that tells the meaning of **soil**. Draw a line under the sentence.

Soil forms a layer on parts of Earth's surface.

Soil forms when weathering breaks down rock. The small pieces of rock form the base of soil. At the same time, dead plants and animals fall to the ground. These once-living things break down into bits. The bits become part of soil, too.

Soil is made of many tiny pieces mixed together.

▶ **What can you observe about this soil?**

____

____

It Takes All Kinds

There are many kinds of soil. Soils can be different colors. Some soils can hold more water than other soils. Some soils are better for growing plants. Sand, humus, and clay are some of the things found in soil. Different amounts of these things make kinds of soil different.

Active Reading

The main idea is the most important idea about something. Draw two lines under the main idea.

Some soil gets very hard when it is dry. The soil in this desert does not hold water well or grow many plants.

Sand is made up of tiny pieces of rock. Sandy soil does not hold water well. Many plants cannot grow in it.

Humus is made of once-living things. Soil that has a lot of humus holds water well and is good for growing many kinds of plants.

Clay is sticky when wet and smooth when dry. Soil that has a lot of clay holds water well but many plants do not grow well in it.

▶ **Circle the picture of the part of soil that helps many kinds of plants grow.**

Sum It Up »

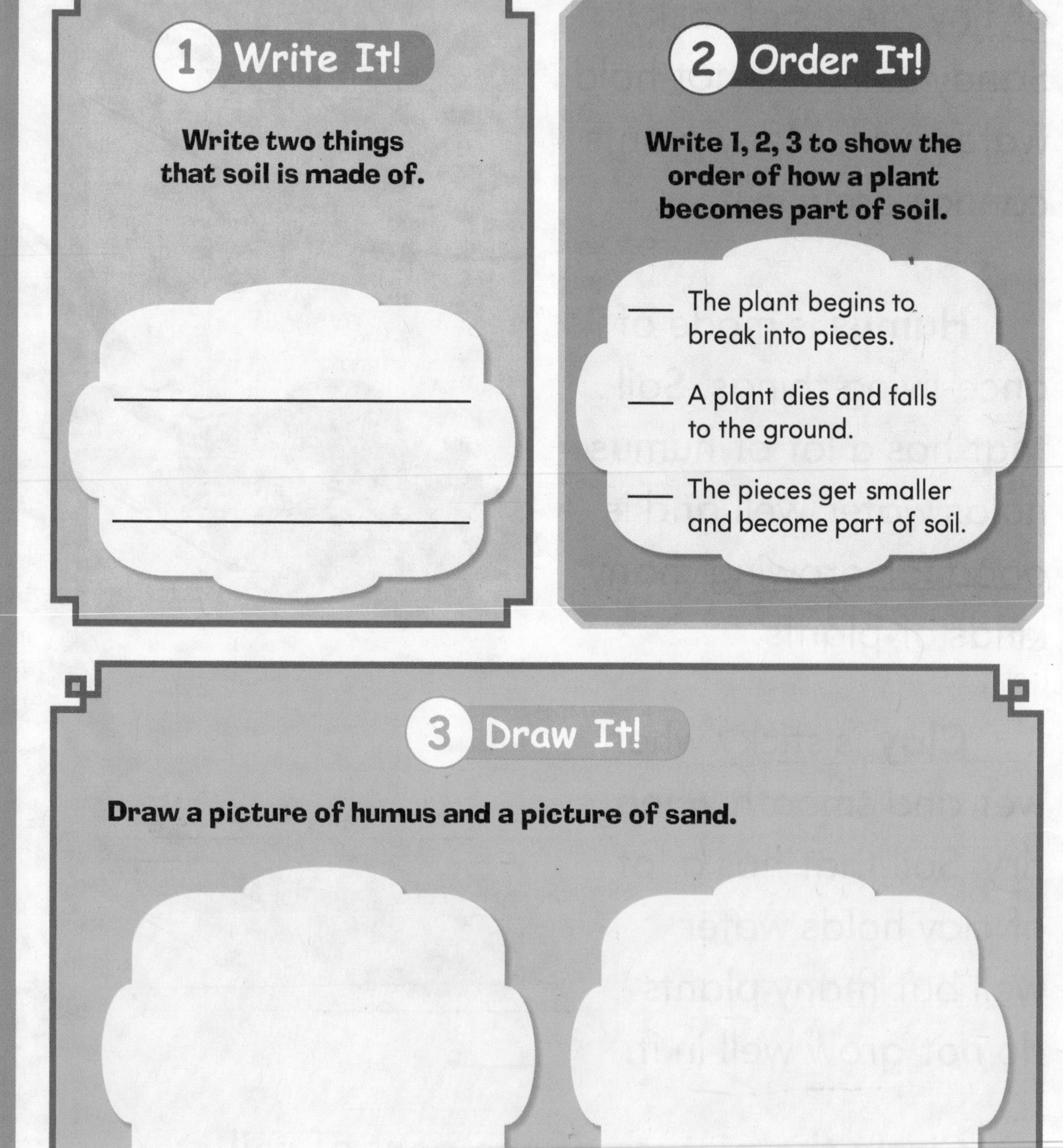

1 Write It!

Write two things that soil is made of.

____

____

2 Order It!

Write 1, 2, 3 to show the order of how a plant becomes part of soil.

___ The plant begins to break into pieces.

___ A plant dies and falls to the ground.

___ The pieces get smaller and become part of soil.

3 Draw It!

Draw a picture of humus and a picture of sand.

Brain Check

Name ______________________

Vocabulary Review

Match each part of soil to its description. Then add another fact about it.

sand

humus

clay

It is sticky when it is wet.

it holds water well

but not good for plants.

It has tiny pieces of rock you can see with your eyes alone.

sandy soil can not hold

water well.

It can hold water well.

It is good for plants.

Apply Concepts

Fill in the chart. Show how soil forms.

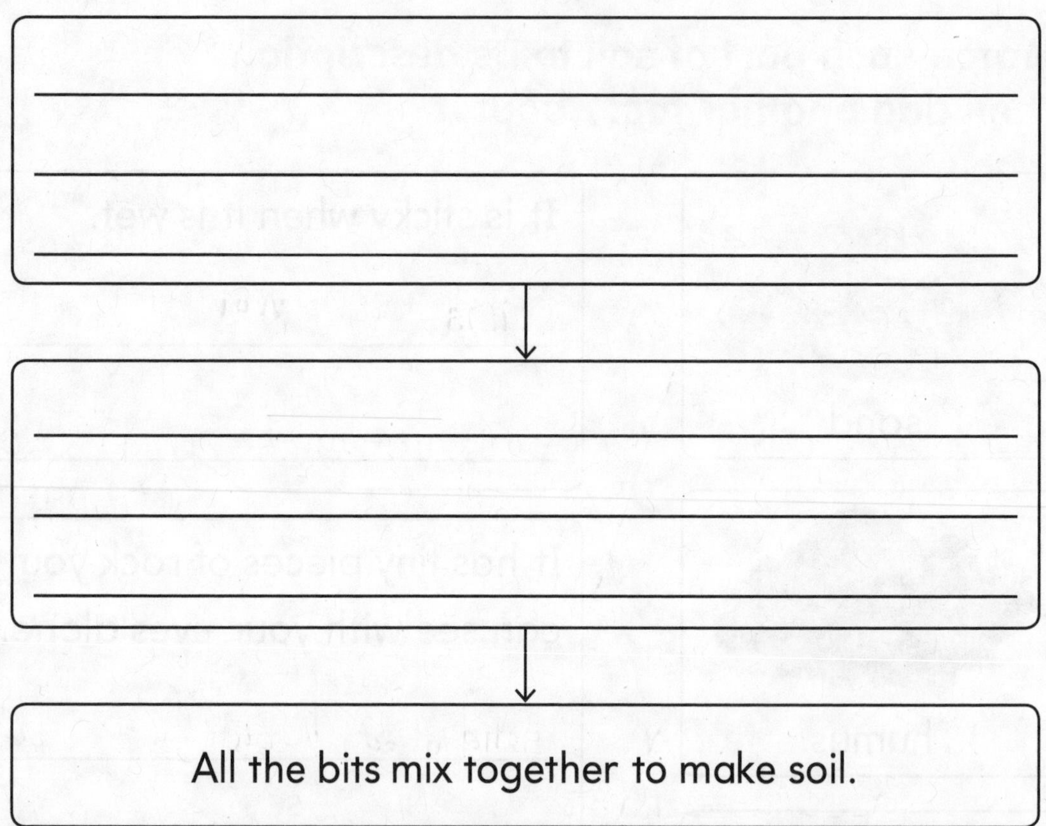

Family Members: Walk with your child near your home to observe soil in your area. Have your child name some properties of the soil.

SC.2.N.1.1 Raise questions ... investigate them in teams ... and generate appropriate explanations based on those explorations. **SC.2.N.1.3** Ask "how do you know?" in appropriate situations .... **SC.2.N.1.5** Distinguish between empirical observation .... and ideas or inferences .... **SC.2.E.6.3** Classify soil types ...

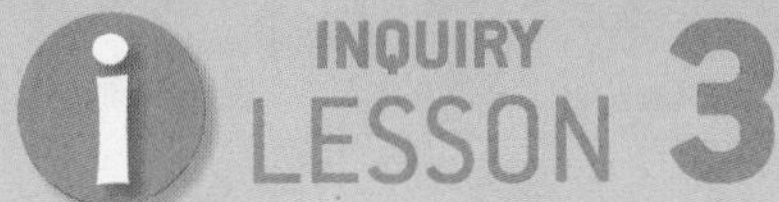

Name ______________________________

Essential Question

How Do Soils Differ?

Materials

three kinds of soil in cups
pencil
bean seeds
water

EXPLORE

You can compare soils in many ways. One way is to find out which soil is best for growing plants.

Before You Begin—Preview the Steps

1. Observe the three soils. How are they different?
2. Use the pencil to make a hole in each soil. Place a seed in each hole. Cover the seeds with soil.
3. Water the soils. Place the cups in a sunny place. Predict what you think will happen.
4. Keep the soils moist. After 1 week, compare the seeds. Which soil was best for growing plants? How do you know?

Set a Purpose

Write what you want to find out.

____

____

Make a Prediction

Predict what you think will happen.

____

____

Think About the Procedure

How will you test the soils?

____

____

____

____

____

____

Name ______________________

ecord Your Data

raw and write to record your observations.

	What does the soil look like?	What happened to the seed after one week?
Soil #1		
Soil #2		
Soil #3		

Claims • Evidence • Reasoning

1. Write a claim about which kind of soil is best for growing plants.

2. What evidence supports your claim?

3. Why does your evidence support your claim?

Ask More Questions

What other questions can you ask about how science tools are used?

Weather

FLORIDA BIG IDEA 7

Earth Systems and Patterns

FLORIDA BIG IDEA 8

Properties of Matter

hurricane, Miami Beach, Florida

I Wonder Why

People prepare for hurricanes. Why? *Turn the page to find out.*

Here's Why

People want to stay safe in case the hurricane causes damage.

Essential Questions and Florida Benchmarks

Science Notebook

Before you begin each lesson, write your thoughts about the Essential Question.

SC.2.E.7.1 Compare and describe changing patterns in nature that repeat themselves, such as weather conditions . . . day to day and season to season. SC.2.E.7.4 Investigate that air is all around us and that moving air is wind. SC.2.P.8.1 Observe and measure objects in terms of their properties, including . . . temperature . . . .

LESSON 1

Essential Question

How Does Weather Change?

Engage Your Brain

Find the answer to the question in the lesson.

When might you see ice on plants?

You might see this in

_______________________________.

Active Reading

Lesson Vocabulary

1. Preview the lesson.
2. Write the 6 vocabulary terms here.

_______________ _______________

_______________ _______________

_______________ _______________

Wonderful Weather

Weather is what the air outside is like. Weather may be sunny, rainy, cloudy, snowy, or windy. It can be hot or cold outside. Weather can change quickly or it can change over many days or months. A weather change that repeats is called a weather pattern.

Active Reading

The main idea is the most important idea about something. Draw a line under the main idea on this page.

You may see thin or puffy clouds on a sunny day. Low, gray clouds usually bring rain.

Clouds help predict weather.

On some days, rain falls.

▶ Draw what the weather is like today.

In some places, the weather gets very cold. Snow may fall.

Measure It!

You can use tools to measure weather. A rain gauge measures precipitation. **Precipitation** is water that falls from the sky. Rain, snow, sleet, and hail are precipitation.

A thermometer measures temperature. **Temperature** is how hot or cold something is.

Active Reading

Find the sentence that tells the meaning of **precipitation**. Draw a line under it.

Air is all around us. Wind is moving air. A weather vane tells the direction of the wind.

This thermometer measures temperature in degrees Fahrenheit and Celsius.

A rain gauge tells how much rain falls.

Do the Math

Measure Temperature

Use a thermometer to measure the temperature of the air in the morning and in the afternoon. Color the pictures below to show the temperatures. Write the temperatures on the lines.

Morning **Afternoon**

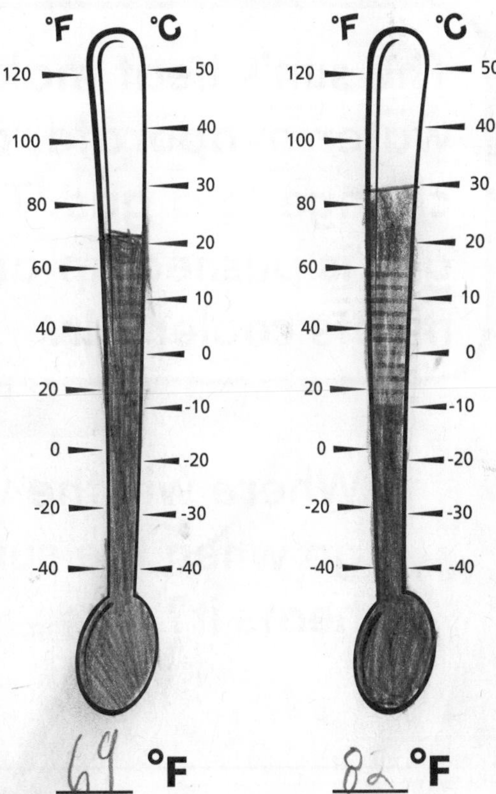

Write a subtraction sentence to find out how the temperature changed.

82°F - 69°F = 13°F

Where Does the Water Go?

The **water cycle** is the way water moves from Earth's surface into the air and back again. The water cycle is a pattern. The water cycle causes weather to change.

The sun's heat makes water evaporate, or change to a gas. The gas is pushed up and meets cooler air.

▶ **Where will the water go when the sun heats it?**

____

____

____

Then the gas cools and condenses, or changes into tiny drops of water. The drops form clouds.

Active Reading

A cause tells why something happens. What causes water drops to fall as rain or snow? Draw one line under the cause.

The water drops join to make bigger ones. The drops fall as precipitation.

The precipitation flows into rivers, lakes, and oceans. Then the water cycle starts again.

Season to Season

A season is a time of year that has a certain kind of weather. Weather changes each season. The seasons always follow the same pattern.

Fabulous Fall

In fall the air outside may be cool. The leaves of some trees change color and drop off.

Wonderful Winter

Winter is the coldest season. Ice can form on land and plants. In some places snow may fall. Winter has the fewest hours of daylight.

Sunny Spring

In spring the air gets warmer. Some places get a lot of rain.

▶ Draw an activity you would do during summer.

Super Summer

Summer is the warmest season. Some places have sudden storms. Summer has the most hours of daylight.

Sum It Up »

1 Draw It!

Draw your favorite kind of weather.

2 Match It!

Match each tool to what it measures.

temperature

rain

3 Complete It!

Fill in the blank.

The movement of water from Earth's surface into the air and back again is called the

_______________.

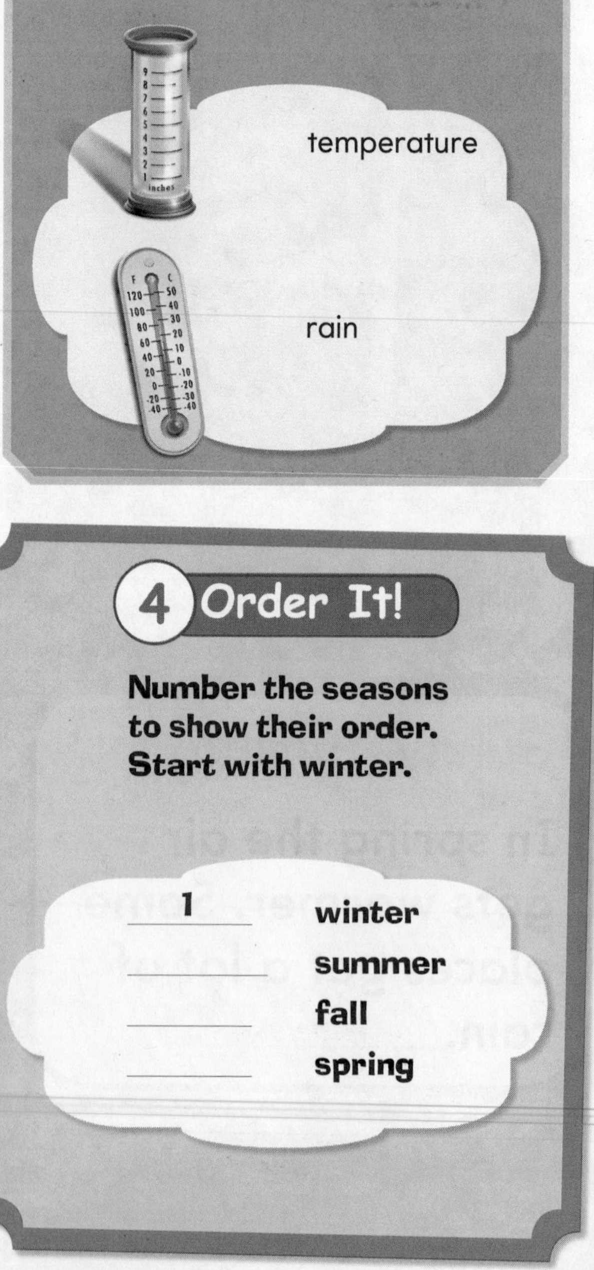

4 Order It!

Number the seasons to show their order. Start with winter.

__1__ **winter**

_____ **summer**

_____ **fall**

_____ **spring**

Name ______________________

Vocabulary Review

Read the clues. Use the words to complete the puzzle.

~~weather~~	~~temperature~~	~~precipitation~~
~~evaporate~~	~~condense~~	

Across

1. The sun's heat can cause water to evaporate.
2. What the air outside is like is called weather.
3. Water can condense into tiny drops.

Down

4. Water that falls as rain or snow is precipitation.
5. Use a thermometer to measure tomperture.

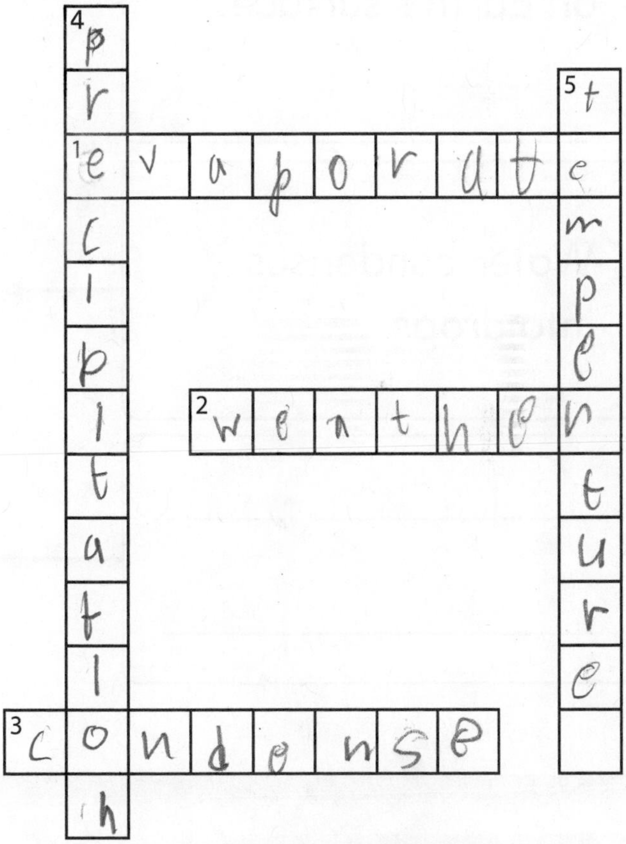

Apply Concepts

Fill in the chart. Show causes and effects in the water cycle.

The Water Cycle

Cause		Effect
The sun heats water on Earth's surface.	→	The water evaporates
Water condenses into drops.	→	It forms a cloud
The cloud gets hevey	→	The drops fall to Earth as rain or snow.

Family Members: See *ScienceSaurus*® for more information about weather.

SC.2.N.1.1 Raise questions ... investigate them in teams ... and generate appropriate explanations based on those explorations. SC.2.N.1.2 Compare the observations made by ... using the same tools. SC.2.N.1.3 Ask "how do you know?" in appropriate situations .... SC.2.E.7.2 Investigate ... that the Sun's energy ... warms the water, land, and air. SC.2.P.8.1 Observe and measure objects in terms of their properties, ...

INQUIRY LESSON 2

Name ____________________

Essential Question

How Does the Sun Heat Earth?

Materials

cup of water
cup of soil
three thermometers

EXPLORE

The sun heats Earth's land, air, and water differently. You can investigate to find out how.

Before You Begin—Preview the Steps

1. Put one thermometer in the cup of water and one in the cup of soil.
2. Put the cups in a sunny spot. Lay the other thermometer next to the cups. Wait about 1 hour.
3. Measure the temperature of the soil, water, and air. Record and compare the temperatures.
4. Compare your observations with those of your classmates.

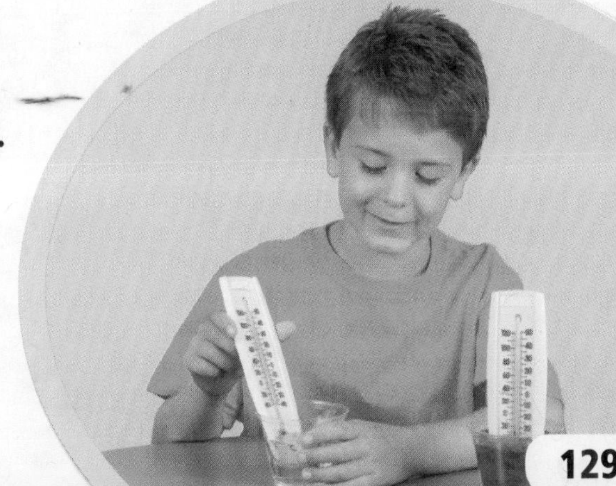

Set a Purpose

Write what you want to find out.

___

___

State Your Hypothesis

Write your hypothesis, or the statement that you will test.

___

___

Think About the Procedure

How will you use the thermometers?

___

___

___

Name ____________________________

Record Your Data

In this chart, record what you observe.

	Starting Temperature	Ending Temperature
air		
water		
soil		

Show your data as a bar graph. Show the starting and the ending temperatures.

Claims • Evidence • Reasoning

1. Write a claim about how the sun heat Earth's land, air, and water.

2. What evidence supports your claim?

3. Why does your evidence support your claim?

Ask More Questions

What other questions can you ask about the sun's heat?

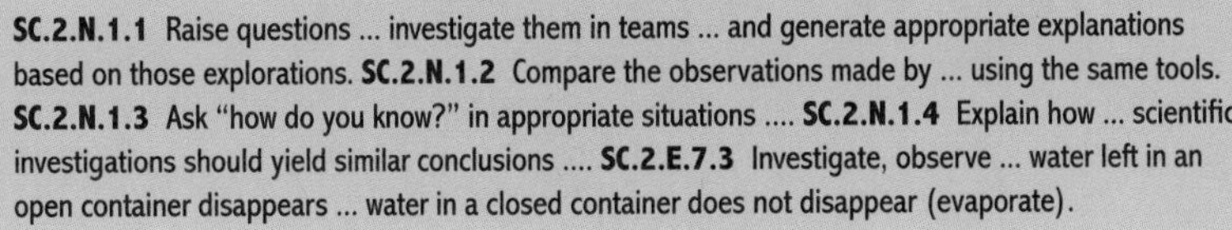
SC.2.N.1.1 Raise questions ... investigate them in teams ... and generate appropriate explanations based on those explorations. **SC.2.N.1.2** Compare the observations made by ... using the same tools. **SC.2.N.1.3** Ask "how do you know?" in appropriate situations .... **SC.2.N.1.4** Explain how ... scientific investigations should yield similar conclusions .... **SC.2.E.7.3** Investigate, observe ... water left in an open container disappears ... water in a closed container does not disappear (evaporate).

Name ____________________________________

:ssential Question

What Is Evaporation?

Materials

measuring cup
water
container with lid
container with no lid

XPLORE

Vhat happens to water you leave in an open container? Investigate to ind out.

Before You Begin—Preview the Steps

1. Pour 1 cup of water into each container. Put the lid on one container.
2. Put the containers in a sunny spot. Wait 1 day.
3. Measure the water in each container. Compare. Which container has more water?
4. Compare your observations with those of your classmates. Repeat the activity. Did you get the same results?

Set a Purpose

Write what you want to find out.

____

____

State Your Hypothesis

Write your hypothesis.

____

____

Think About the Procedure

1. Why should both containers start with the same amount of water?

____

____

____

2. Why does one container have a lid?

____

____

Name ______________________

Record Your Data

Record what you observe.

	How much water?	
	Before	After
Container with a Lid		
Container with No Lid		

Show your data as a bar graph. Show the amounts of water before and after.

Claims • Evidence • Reasoning

1. Write a claim about whether water evaporates from an open container.

2. What evidence supports your claim?

3. Why does your evidence support your claim?

Ask More Questions

What other questions can you ask about evaporation?

SC.2.E.7.5 State the importance of preparing for severe weather, lightning, and other weather related events.

LESSON 4

Essential Question

How Can We Prepare for Severe Weather?

Engage Your Brain

Find the answer to the question in the lesson.

When can wind take the shape of a cone?

when there is a

____

Active Reading

Lesson Vocabulary

1. Preview the lesson.
2. Write the 4 vocabulary terms here.

______________ ______________

______________ ______________

Wild Weather

Sometimes weather gets wild! Then we have severe, or very bad, weather. A thunderstorm is one kind of severe weather. A **thunderstorm** is a storm with a lot of rain, thunder, and lightning.

Active Reading

A detail is a fact about a main idea. Draw one line under a detail. Draw an arrow to the main idea it tells about.

Lightning is a flash of electricity in the sky.

A tornado is a kind of severe weather, too. A **tornado** is a spinning cloud with a cone shape. A tornado has very strong winds.

Another kind of severe weather is a hurricane. A **hurricane** is a large storm with heavy rain and strong winds.

▶ **What weather does this picture show? Label it.**

____

A hurricane can cause a lot of damage to an area.

Why It Matters

Safety First

Storms can be dangerous. Scientists called meteorologists predict storms. They warn people about storms. Then people can do things to stay safe and be prepared for storms.

Meteorologists use tools such as computers to help predict and track severe weather.

▶ What might happen if meteorologists couldn't predict weather in your area?

____

____

People try to protect property from severe weather.

Tips for Storm Safety

Read these tips on how to get ready for a storm. Then add your own tip at the bottom.

1. Get extra food and water.
2. Get other things you may need, such as flashlights and blankets.
3. Make a plan for your family and pets.
4. Stay inside.
5. ______________________
____
____

Sum It Up »

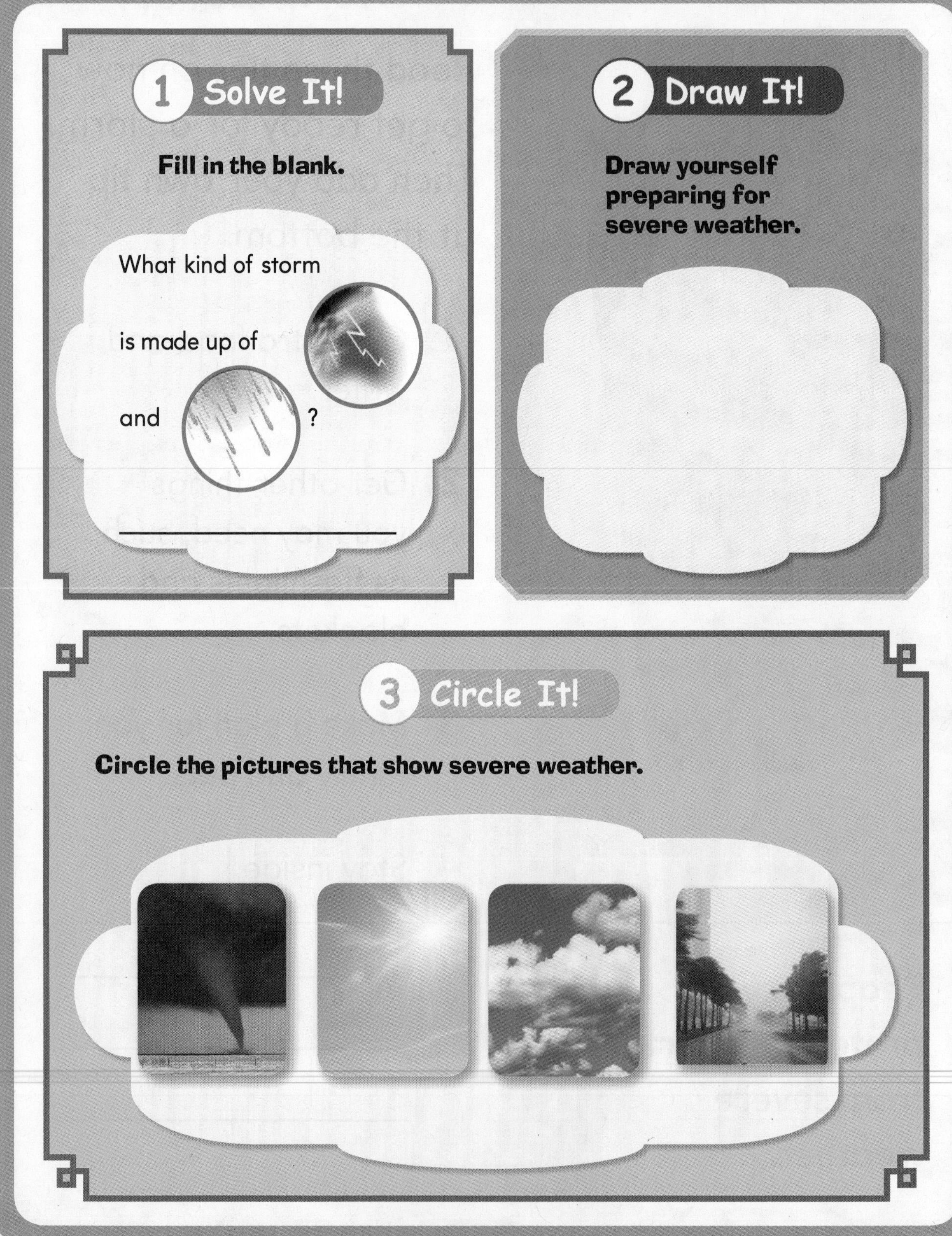

1 Solve It!

Fill in the blank.

What kind of storm

is made up of [lightning picture]

and [rain picture] ?

____

2 Draw It!

Draw yourself preparing for severe weather.

3 Circle It!

Circle the pictures that show severe weather.

Brain Check

LESSON **4**

Name ______________________

Vocabulary Review

Find each word in the puzzle. Then answer the questions.

thunderstorm **hurricane** **lightning** **tornado**

q	i	g	g	d	o	r	a	s	t	i	e
t	h	u	n	d	e	r	s	t	o	r	m
l	s	j	k	d	a	z	y	l	r	p	a
e	v	h	u	r	r	i	c	a	n	e	m
w	a	t	r	s	p	l	i	t	a	r	f
b	w	e	g	l	n	o	w	t	d	u	i
l	i	g	h	t	n	i	n	g	o	r	b

1. What might you see during a thunderstorm?

____

____

2. What kind of storm always has heavy rain and strong winds?

____

Apply Concepts

How would you prepare for severe weather in your area? Write a plan.

Family Members: Work with your child to make a storm safety plan for your family.

Ask a Storm Chaser

What kinds of storms do storm chasers look for?
Most storm chasers look for tornadoes. A few storm chasers look for hurricanes.

How do you work?
Storm chasers watch the weather carefully. We learn about bad storms. We try to predict where to find them. Then we drive to see a storm.

How does storm chasing help other people?
Most storm chasers work with weather centers. If we spot a storm, we can alert the police and people on farms.

Now It's Your Turn!

▶ What question would you ask a storm chaser?

____

____

Safety from the Storm

▶ **Draw or write the answer to each question to get to safety.**

1. Your family has a storm kit. You use it if you lose power or get hurt. Draw one thing you would put in a storm kit.
2. A storm might be coming. Why should you make a plan?
3. Storm chasers spot a tornado. Draw a picture of what they might see.
4. Tornado warning! Your family follows its safety plan by finding shelter. Why?

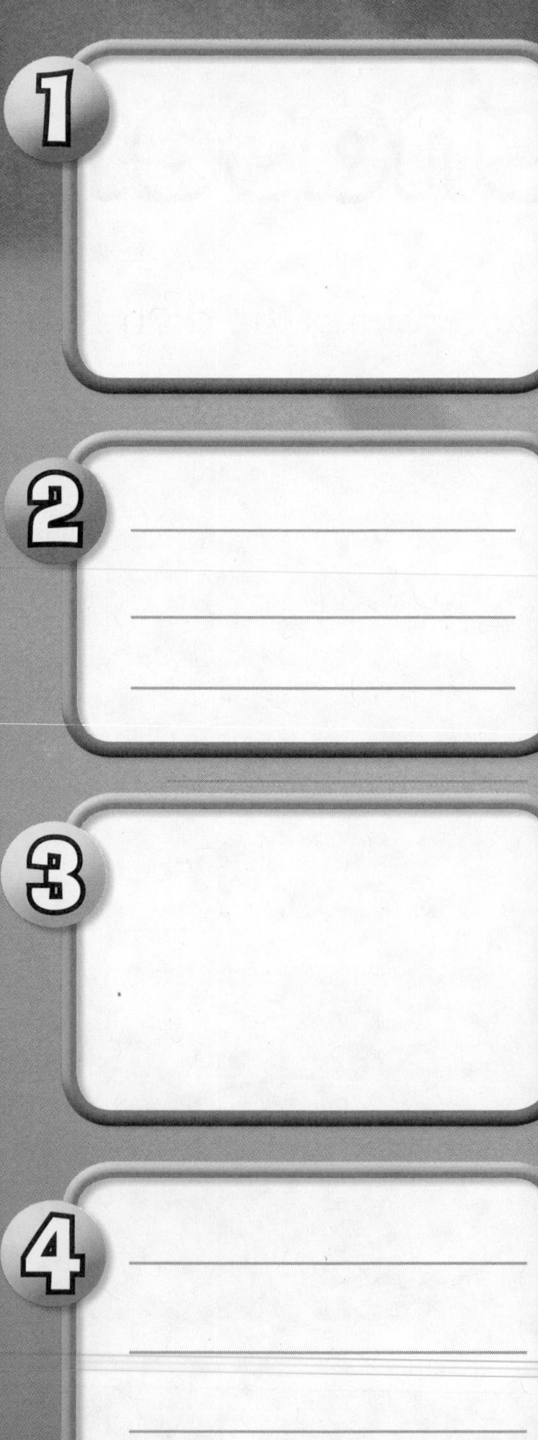

SC.2.N.1.1 Raise questions about the natural world, investigate them in teams... and generate appropriate explanations. **SC.2.N.1.2** Compare the observations made by different groups using the same tools. **SC.2.N.1.6** Explain how scientists alone or in groups are always investigating new ways to solve problems. **SC.2.E.7.1** Compare and describe changing patterns in nature that repeat themselves, such as weather conditions...

S.T.E.M.

ENGINEERING  TECHNOLOGY

Watching Weather

Hurricane Airplanes

Hurricane airplanes collect data about hurricanes. The data help scientists predict and track hurricanes.

The airplane flies close to a hurricane.

Weather tools are placed in tubes. The plane drops the tubes into the hurricane.

The tubes fall into the center of the hurricane. The tools in the tubes collect storm data.

S.T.E.M. (continued)

Weather Technology

Look at the diagram of the weather tube. Then answer the questions.

The parachute slows down the tube as it falls through the hurricane.

The tube holds weather tools. The tools collect data about wind speed and temperature.

What might happen if the parachute did not open?

____

____

____

____

____

Improvise It:

Weather Station

Suppose you want to give a weather report to your class each day. You could build a weather station to collect data. What weather tools will you need?

▶ A weather report tells about the temperature and wind and if it is rainy or sunny.

S.T.E.M. (continued)

What to Do:

1. Think of the type of data you will collect.

2. Make or gather the weather tools you need.

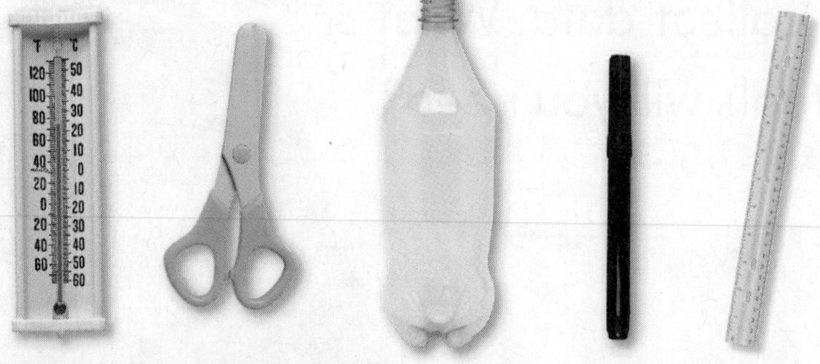

3. Build and test your weather station.

4. Record your data. Report to the class.

5. Draw and write about your weather station data in your Science Notebook.

All About Matter

tubing in Florida

I Wonder Why

The tubes keep their shapes. Why? *Turn the page to find out.*

Here's Why

Gases take the shape of their container.

Essential Questions and Florida Benchmarks

Science Notebook

Before you begin each lesson, write your thoughts about the Essential Question.

SC.2.P.8.1 Observe and measure objects in terms of their properties, including size, shape, color . . . weight, texture, sinking or floating in water . . . .

LESSON 1

Essential Question

What Are Properties of Matter?

Engage Your Brain

Look closely at the picture. Find the answer to the question in the lesson.

What is this a picture of?

It is ______________.

Active Reading

Lesson Vocabulary

1. Preview the lesson.
2. Write the 5 vocabulary terms here.

______________ ______________

______________ ______________

______________ ______________

It All Matters

Objects around you are made of matter. **Matter** is anything that takes up space.

Matter has properties. A **property** is one part of what something is like. You can tell about objects by their properties. Some properties are size, shape, and color.

▶ **Draw objects with different shapes on the bookshelves.**

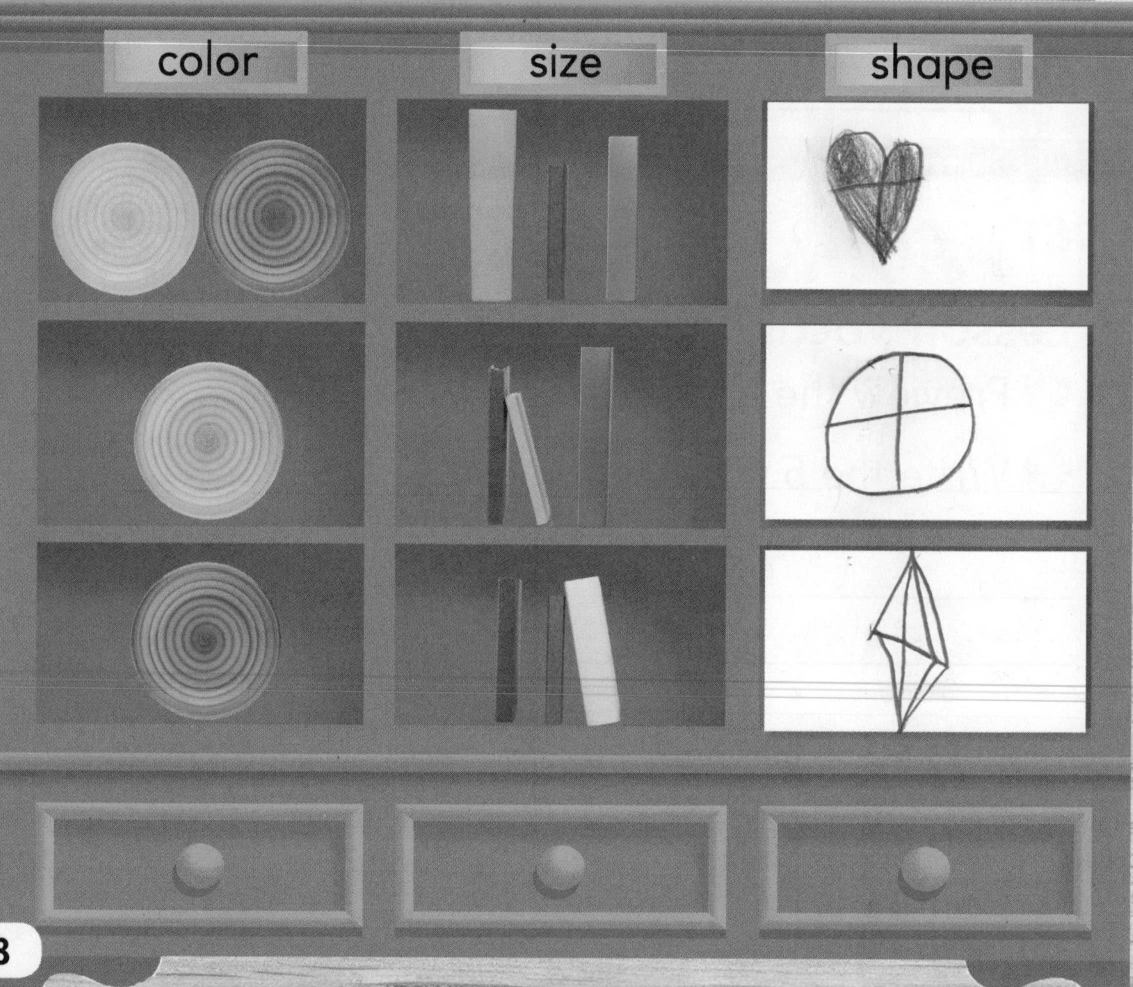

Keep in Touch

Texture is another property of matter. **Texture** is the way something feels. The floor is hard. The cat's fur is soft. They have different textures. What other things feel hard or soft? What other words tell about texture?

Active Reading

Draw a line under the sentence that tells the meaning of **texture.**

▶ Draw something hard. ▶ Draw something soft.

The floor is smooth, but the lamp shade is rough.

Measure Up!

You **measure** to find out about the size, weight, or amount of things.

Suppose you want to know the length of an object, or how long it is. You can measure length with a ruler, a meterstick, or a tape measure.

Do the Math

Measure Length

Use a ruler to measure the lengths of objects. Write the names of three objects. Record the lengths in inches. Circle the name of the shortest object.

Length of Classroom Objects	
Object	**Length in Inches**

Worth the Weight

Why is it hard to lift a efrigerator? A refrigerator s heavy! An egg is easy to lift because it is light. **Weight** is a neasure of how heavy something eels. A scale is used to measure he weight of an object.

▶ **Draw a line from each fruit to the word that tells about its weight.**

Light

Heavy

What Floats? What Sinks?

Look at the objects in the tub. The rubber duck floats. It stays on top of the water. The soap sinks. It falls to the bottom of the water. Which other objects in the tub float? Which other ones sink?

Active Reading

Opposites are words for things that are very different, such as light and heavy or stop and go. Draw triangles around two words on this page that are opposites.

▶ Draw an object that floats.

▶ Draw an object that sinks.

This tub is full of things that sink and float.

Sum It Up »

1 Mark It!

Sort by properties. Draw an X on the object in each group that does not belong.

2 Circle It!

Circle the objects that sink.

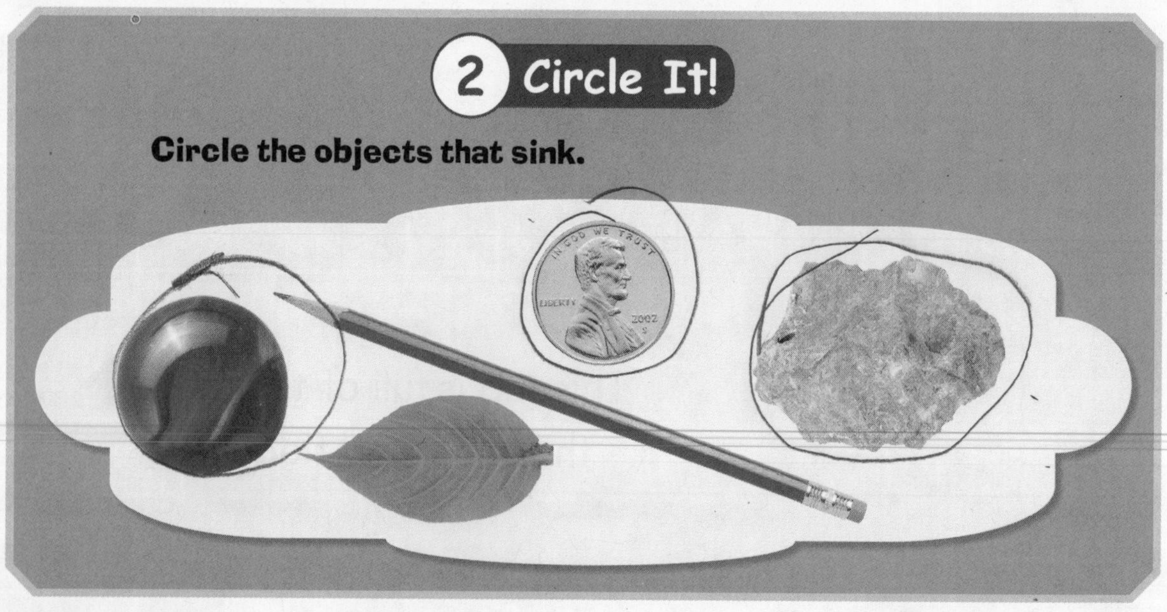

Brain Check

Name ______________________

Vocabulary Review

Sort the words in the word bank. Write them in the chart. Show which words tell about each property of matter.

Properties of Matter

hard	heavy	round	small	soft
black	red	big	square	light

Size	Shape	Color	Texture	Weight
big Small	round squar	black red	hard soft	heavy light

Apply Concepts

Tell about the properties of the beach ball.
Write a word on each line to complete the word web.

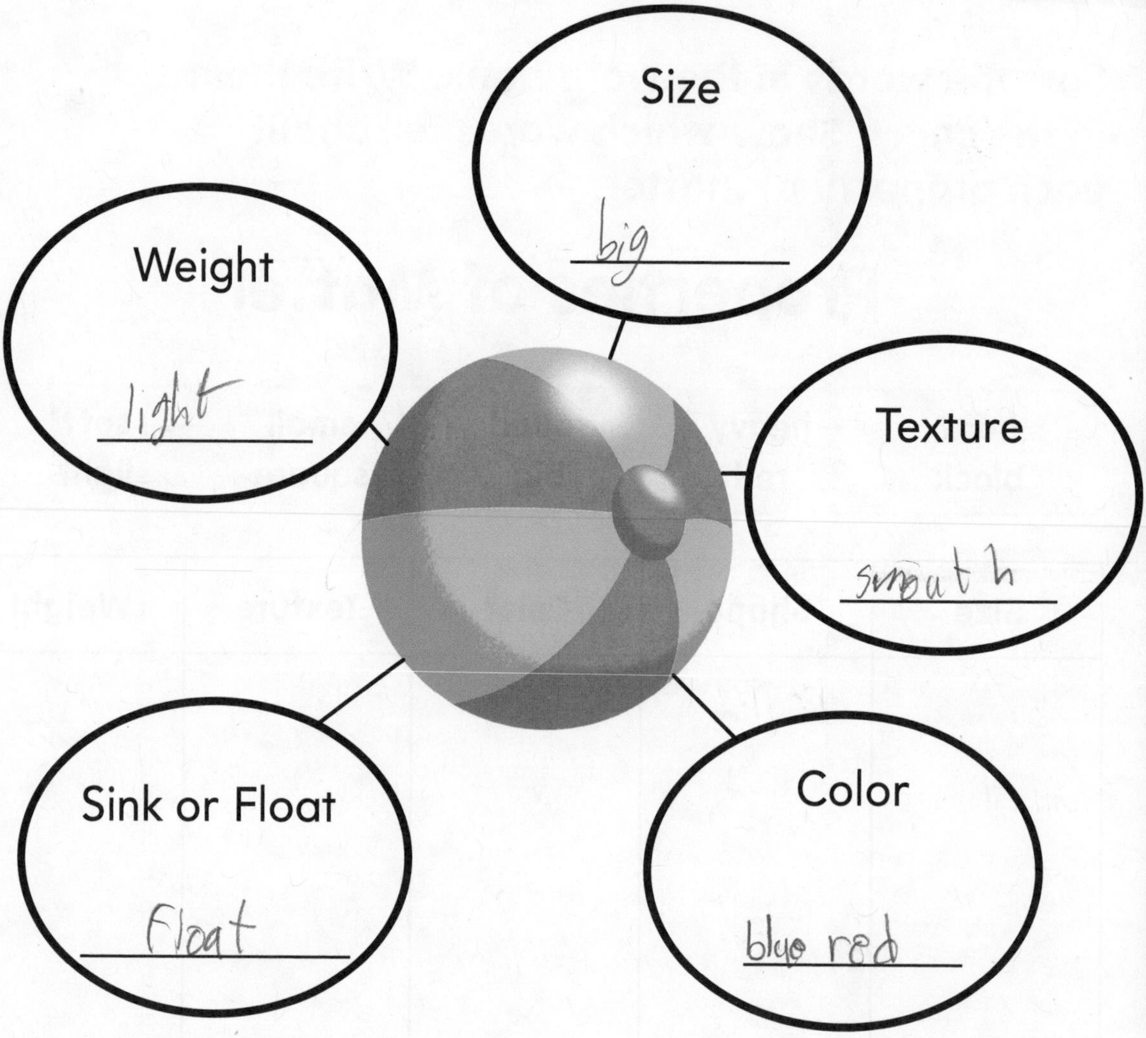

Size
big

Weight
light

Texture
smouth

Sink or Float
Float

Color
blue red

Family Members: See *ScienceSaurus*® for more information about matter.

SC.2.N.1.1 Raise questions ... investigate them in teams ... and generate appropriate explanations based on those explorations. SC.2.N.1.2 Compare the observations made by ... using the same tools. SC.2.N.1.3 Ask "how do you know?" in appropriate situations. ... SC.2.N.1.4 Explain how ... scientific investigations should yield similar conclusions ... SC.2.P.8.1 Observe and measure objects in terms of their properties, including size ... weight ....

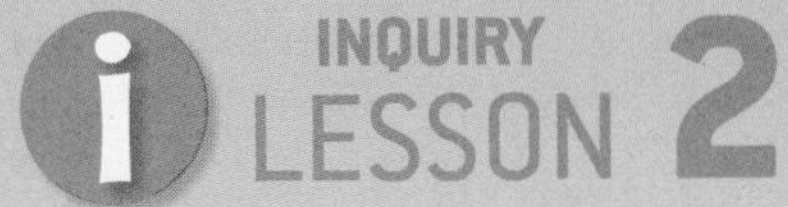

Name ____________________

Essential Question

How Can We Measure and Compare Objects?

Materials

large classroom objects
ruler or meterstick
scale

EXPLORE

You can measure length using a ruler or a meterstick. You can measure weight by using a scale. Use these tools to measure and compare some classroom objects.

Before You Begin—Preview the Steps

1. Measure the length of each object. Order the objects from shortest to longest.
2. Measure the weight of the same three objects. Order them from lightest to heaviest.
3. Compare the order for your two groups of measurements. Are they the same or different?
4. Repeat the activity. Did you get the same results? Compare with classmates.

Set a Purpose

Write what you will do in this investigation.

Think About the Procedure

1. How will you measure length? How will you measure weight?

2. Why will you repeat the measurements?

Name ______________________

Record Your Data

Record your results in the charts below. Remember to order the lengths from shortest to longest. Order the weights from lightest to heaviest.

Object	Length

Object	Weight

Claims • Evidence • Reasoning

1. Write a claim about whether longer objects are heavier than shorter objects.

2. What evidence supports your claim?

3. Why does your evidence support your claim?

Ask More Questions

What other questions can you ask about how to measure and compare objects?

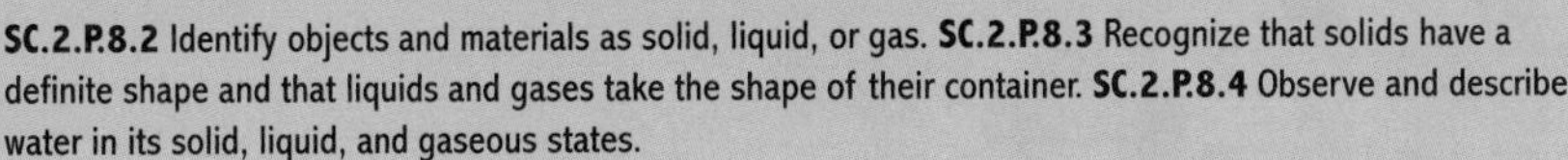

SC.2.P.8.2 Identify objects and materials as solid, liquid, or gas. **SC.2.P.8.3** Recognize that solids have a definite shape and that liquids and gases take the shape of their container. **SC.2.P.8.4** Observe and describe water in its solid, liquid, and gaseous states.

LESSON 3

Essential Question

What Are Solids, Liquids, and Gases?

Engage Your Brain

Find the answer to the question in the lesson.

What is inside the balloon?

____

Active Reading

Lesson Vocabulary

1 Preview the lesson.

2 Write the 5 vocabulary terms here.

______________ ______________

______________ ______________

______________ ______________

Matter Matters

You know that matter is anything that takes up space. Some things have more matter than others. **Mass** is the amount of matter in an object. This boy has more mass than his beach ball.

Solid, liquid, and gas are three states of matter. The boy's sunglasses are a solid. The water in his bottle is a liquid. The beach ball is filled with gases.

Active Reading

Find the sentence that tells the meaning of **mass**. Draw a line under the sentence.

What two states of matter make up the beach ball?

Solid as a Rock

Look at the chair, the towel, and the hat. How are these objects the same? The answer is that all three are solids.

A **solid** is the only state of matter that has its own shape. What other solids do you see in this picture?

▶ **Draw a solid object that you would take to the beach.**

Shape Up!

Is orange juice a solid? No. It does not have its own shape. If you pour juice from a pitcher in to a glass, its shape changes.

Juice is a liquid. A **liquid** is a state of matter that takes the shape of its container. What other liquids can you name?

▶ **Color the empty glass to show the shape the liquid would take in it.**

Salt water is a kind of liquid.

Life's a Gas

This girl is blowing air into the beach ball. Air is made up of gases. A **gas** is a state of matter that fills all the space in its container. The air will keep spreading out until it fills the entire beach ball.

Active Reading

Find the sentence that tells the meaning of **gas**. Draw a line under the sentence.

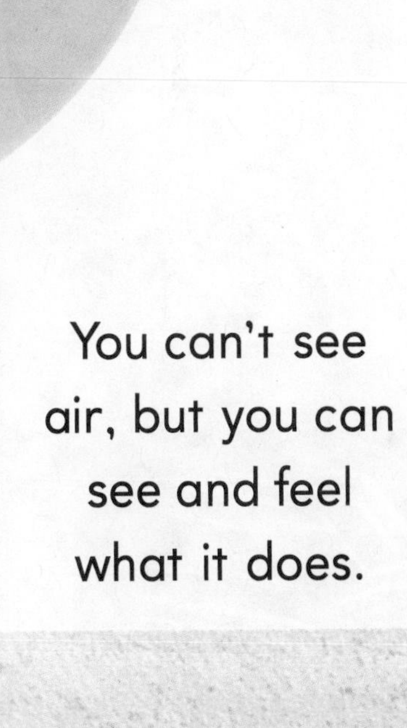

You can't see air, but you can see and feel what it does.

Wonderful Water

On the outside of th glass, water vapor is becoming liquid water.

There are three states of water—solid, liquid, and gas. The water we drink is a liquid. Solid water is ice. Water in the form of a gas is **water vapor**.

You can't see it, but water vapor is in the air around this glass.

▶ **What is water vapor?**

Water Vapor is Water in a form of an gas

States of Water

Write in each empty box to complete the chart.

Name	State	Shape
ice	solid	has its own shape.
water	liquid	takes the shape of its container
Water Vapor	gas	fills up all the space in a container

Sum It Up »

1 Color It!

Color the solids red. Color the liquids blue. Color the gases yellow.

2 Write It!

Answer the question.
What do you call the three states of water?

____

Brain Check

Name ______________________

Vocabulary Review

Write the word for each clue. Fill in the missing numbers in the table. Then decode the message.

a	b	c	d	e	f	g	h	i	j	k	l	m
11	26	4	16	8	25	9	13	23	6	14	20	19

n	o	p	q	r	s	t	u	v	w	x	y	z
7	18	1	3	22	21	17	10	15	10	5	12	24

takes the shape of its container L I q u i d
20 23 3 2 23 16

water in the form of a gas v a p o r
15 11 1 18 22

amount of matter in an object M a s s
19 11 21 21

fills all the space of its container g a s
9 11 21

u d u y u t t h e
11 16 11 12 11 17 17 13 8

___ ___ ___ ___ ___ ___ ___ ___
26 8 11 4 13 23 21 11

___ ___ ___ ___ ___ ___ ___ ___ ___ ___ ___ ___ ___ ___!
20 11 2 9 13 23 7 9 19 11 17 17 8 22

Apply Concepts

Write or draw to fill in the chart with examples of solids, liquids, and gases.

Solids, Liquids, and Gases

Solids	Liquids	Gases

Family Members: As you and your child walk around your home, point out objects and materials. Have your child classify each one as a solid, a liquid, or a gas.

Get to Know...
Dr. Mario Molina

Dr. Mario Molina is a chemist, or a person who studies the properties of substances and how they interact. For many years he studied materials called chlorofluorocarbons (CFCs). CFCs were used in spray cans and refrigerators. Dr. Molina found that CFCs harm the ozone layer, a layer of gas around Earth. The ozone layer protects us from the sun's harmful rays.

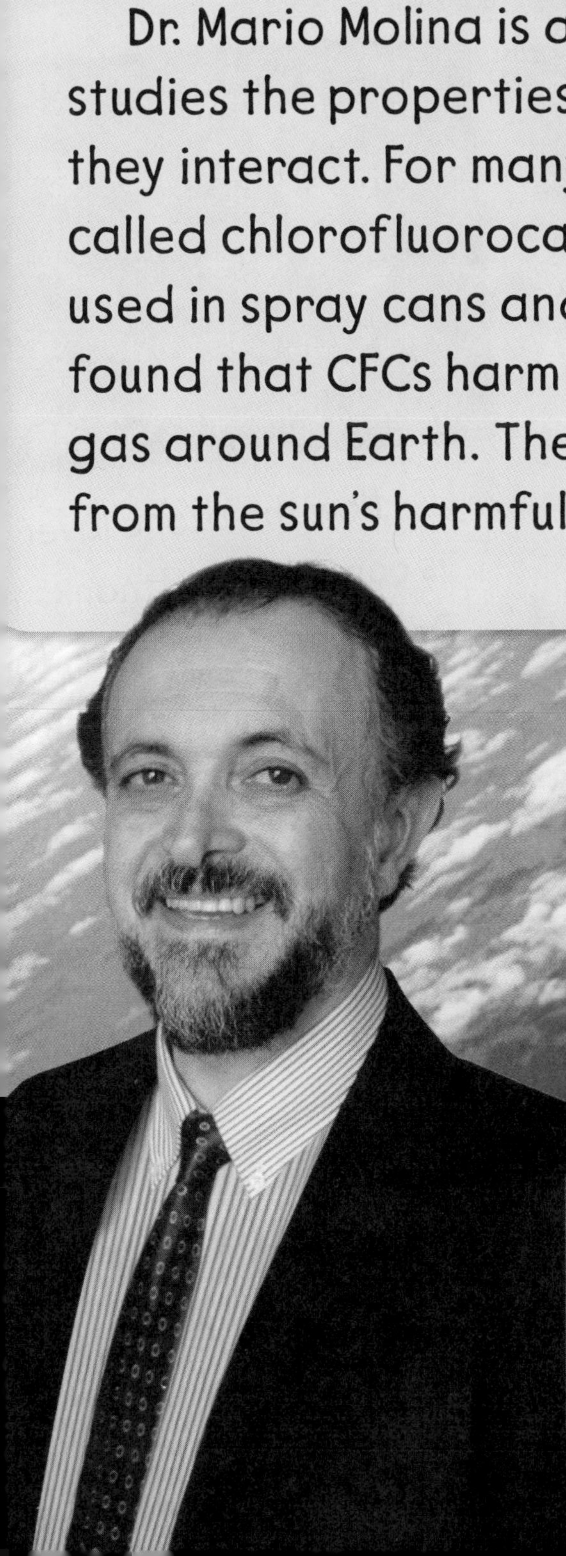

...Fun Fact

When Dr. Molina was a boy, he used a microscope to look at very tiny living things like this one.

This Leads to That

Dr. Molina and other scientists talked to lawmakers. They worked to get rid of CFCs in spray cans.

Now the ozone layer is coming back, thanks t[o] Dr. Molina and others. In 1995, Dr. Molina won the Nobel Prize for his work.

▶ How did Dr. Molina's work help the environment?

____

____

SC.2.N.1.1 Raise questions ... investigate them in teams ... and generate appropriate explanations based on those explorations. SC.2.N.1.2 Compare the observations made by different groups using the same tools. SC.2.P.8.6 Measure and compare the volume of liquids using containers of various shapes and sizes.

Name ______________________________

ssential Question

How Can We Compare Volumes?

Materials

containers of various sizes and shapes

water

marker

measuring cup

XPLORE

How much water is in each container? Investigate to find out.

Before You Begin—Preview the Steps

1. Observe the 3 containers your teacher filled with water. Draw a line to show where the water level is on each container.

2. Pour the water from one of the containers into a measuring cup. Record the amount. Pour the water back into the same container.

3. Repeat Step 2 for the other two containers. Compare the numbers.

4. Compare your results with your classmates.

Set a Purpose

Write what you will do in this investigation.

The purpose is to measure, record, and compar the volium of wa in 3 different shaped containers.

State Your Hypothesis

Write your hypothesis, or the statement that you will test.

I think that the water in the rectangular container

Think About the Procedure

How will you figure out which container is holding the most water?.

We will pour the water into a measuring cup to figure out the volume of water in each container.

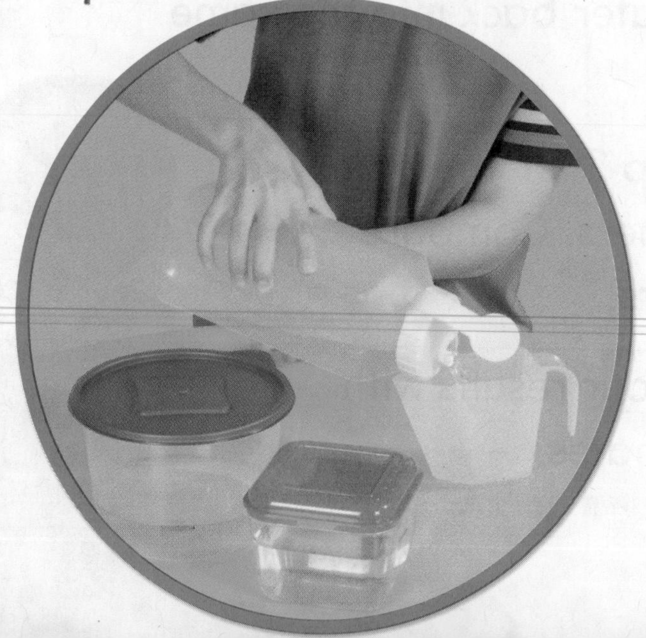

Name ______________________

Record Your Data

In the chart, draw the shape of each container. Write in the amount that each container held.

Shape of Container	Amount of Water
	200 ml
	125 ml
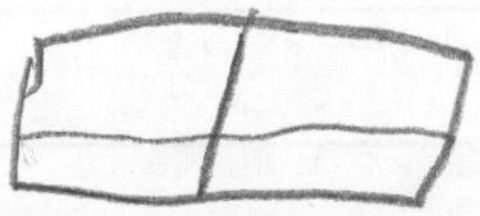	225

Show your data in a bar graph.

Claims • Evidence • Reasoning

1. Write a claim about whether the tallest container holds the most water.

2. What evidence supports your claim?

3. Why does your evidence support your claim?

Ask More Questions

What other questions can you ask about volume?

SC.2.N.1.1 Raise questions ... investigate them in teams ... and generate appropriate explanations based on those explorations. SC.2.N.1.2 Compare the observations made ... using the same tools. SC.2.N.1.6 Explain how scientists ... solve problems.

S.T.E.M.

ENGINEERING & TECHNOLOGY

Kitchen Technology

Cooking Tools

The tools you use to cook are technology. They are designed to help you in the kitchen! A spoon is technology. So is an oven.

Whole Wheat Chocolate Chip Cookies

2 cups whole wheat flour
1 egg
1 teaspoon vanilla
1 teaspoon baking soda

A recipe tells you how to make food.

Measuring cups and spoons use standard units to measure ingredients.

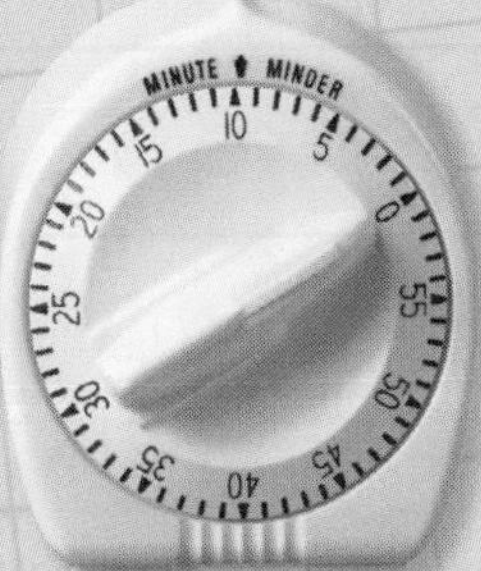

A timer tells you when something has finished baking.

S.T.E.M. (continued)

Make Do

Write to tell how you would solve each problem.

1. You are baking muffins. The timer on your oven is broken! How else could you measure how long to bake the muffins?

____

____

____

2. You need 3 cups of flour for a recipe. You only have a 1-cup measuring cup. How could you use it to measure the flour?

____

____

____

____

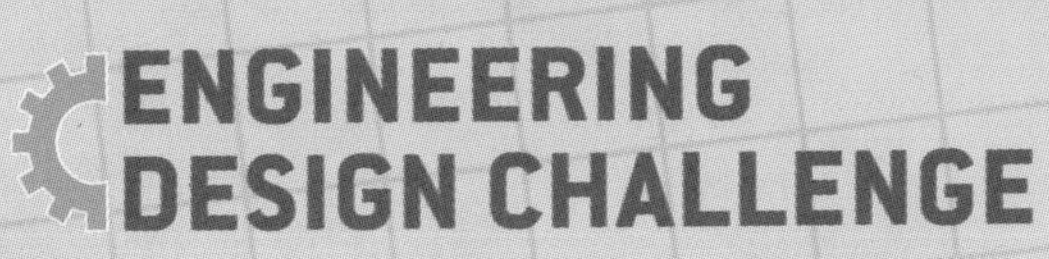

Think About Process:

Write a Recipe

What is your favorite sandwich? How do you make it? What tools do you use? Write a recipe that tells how to make your sandwich.

cooking tools

recipe

Homemade Peanut Butter

2 cups (500 ml) unsalted roasted peanuts

1 tablespoon (15 ml) vegetable oil

S.T.E.M. (continued)

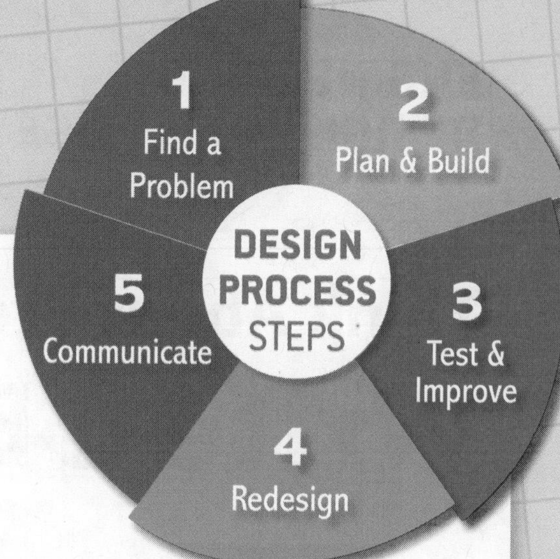

What to Do:

1. List the ingredients and tools you need.
2. What steps will you follow?
3. Test your recipe.
4. Think of ways to improve your recipe.
5. Write about your recipe in your Science Notebook.

Matter Can Change

Florida oranges

Changes in Matter

I Wonder How

The oranges have been changed. How?
Turn the page to find out.

Here's How

Cutting an orange changes its size and shape. Squeezing an orange causes its juice to come out. Freezing the juice changes it from a liquid to a solid.

Essential Questions and Florida Benchmarks

Science Notebook

Before you begin each lesson, write your thoughts about the Essential Question.

SC.2.P.9.1 Investigate that materials can be altered to change some of their properties, but not all materials respond the same way to any one alteration.

LESSON 1

Essential Question

How Does Matter Change?

Engage Your Brain

Use words from the lesson to answer the question.

How does the artist make this sculpture?

She ______ water and then ______ the ice.

Active Reading

Lesson Vocabulary

1. Preview the lesson.
2. Write the 4 vocabulary terms here.

______________ ______________

______________ ______________

Deep Freeze

Think about making juice pops. You put juice in a freezer. The juice **freezes**, or turns from a liquid to a solid. You take the solid juice pops out of the freezer. They **melt**, or change to a liquid.

Not all things freeze or melt at the same temperature. Some liquids won't freeze in a freezer. A plastic bag won't melt if you leave it out of a freezer.

Active Reading

When you contrast, you tell ways in which things are different. Draw triangles around two words that are being contrasted.

This ice cream is frozen solid.

▶ Draw something that melts.

1 2 3 Do the Math

Compare Numbers

Circle the answers.

Ice cream melts faster when the air temperature is higher.

At which temperature will ice cream melt faster?

75 °F or **45 °F**

50 °F or **85 °F**

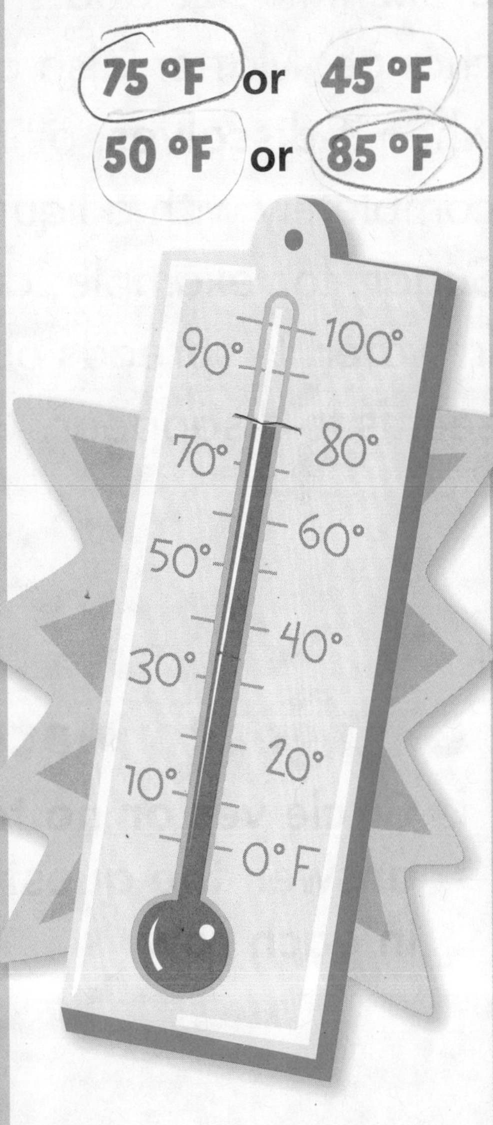

The ice cream melted, but the nuts and cherry did not melt.

Time for a Change

When matter is cut or broken, its size and shape change. Matter also changes when it **dissolves**, or mixes completely with a liquid. Sugar, for example, dissolves in water. It spreads out and seems to disappear.

Changes to Matter

▶ Circle yes or no to answer the question in each row.

Can you dissolve it in water?

lemonade powder and sugar

(yes) no

Can you cut it?

apple

(yes) no

Can you break it?

egg

(yes) no

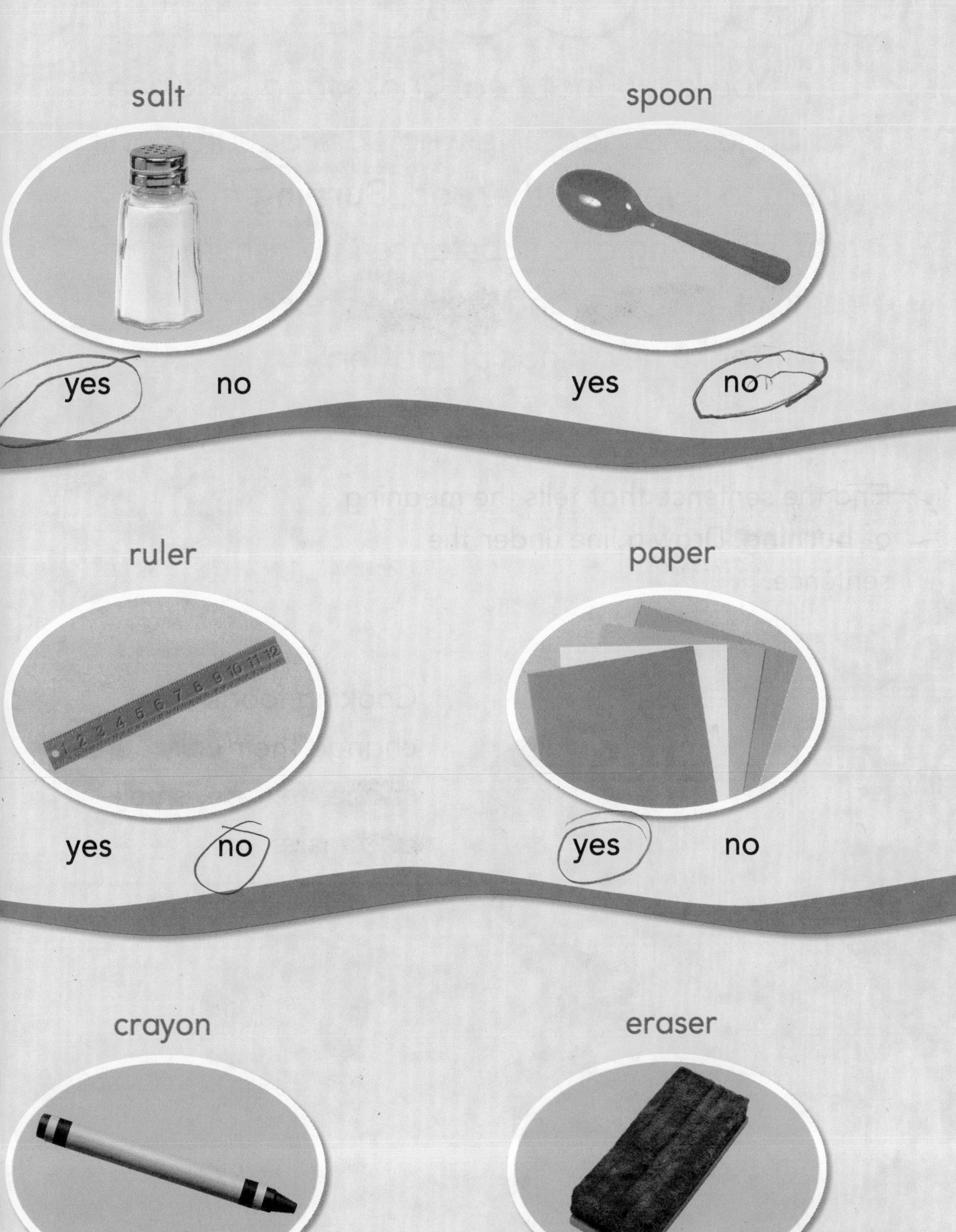
salt
yes
no
spoon
yes
no
ruler
1 2 3 4 5 6 7 8 9 10 11 12
yes
no
paper
yes
no
crayon
yes
no
eraser
yes
no

Get Cooking

You know that heat cooks food. Cooking changes the food. The wood or coals in a grill burn to help cook the food. **Burning** means the changing of a substance into ashes and smoke. Cooking and burning are changes that make new kinds of matter.

Active Reading

Find the sentence that tells the meaning of **burning**. Draw a line under the sentence.

Cooking foods can change their color, size, shape, texture, smell, and taste.

▶ **Write the change that is happening in each picture.**

Burning

cooking

Sum It Up »

1 Circle It!
One picture shows a new kind of matter being made. Circle it.
CH
2 Draw It!
Draw something before and after it melts.

Name ________________________

Vocabulary Review

Read the label in each box. Write or draw two things you can change that way.

Answer the question.

What do burning and cooking do to matter?

cange it

permanently

Apply Concepts

In each box, write a word that tells the cause of the effect.

	Cause	Effect
juice pop	melting	juice
lemonade powder and sugar mixed in water	dissolve	lemonade
water	frese	ice

Family Members: See *ScienceSaurus®* for more information about matter.

SC.2.N.1.1 Raise questions ... investigate them in teams ... and generate appropriate explanations based on those explorations. **SC.2.N.1.2** Compare the observations made ... using the same tools. **SC.2.N.1.6** Explain how scientists ... solve problems. **SC.2.P.9.1** Investigate that materials can be altered to change some of their properties, but not all materials respond the same way to any one alteration.

S.T.E.M.

ENGINEERING & TECHNOLOGY

Cross That Bridge

Materials Matter

People combine materials to build things. When put together, the materials do things that they cannot do alone. Look at the Brooklyn Bridge. It was built with stone and steel. Stone was used because it is strong and lasts a long time. Steel was used because it is strong and flexible.

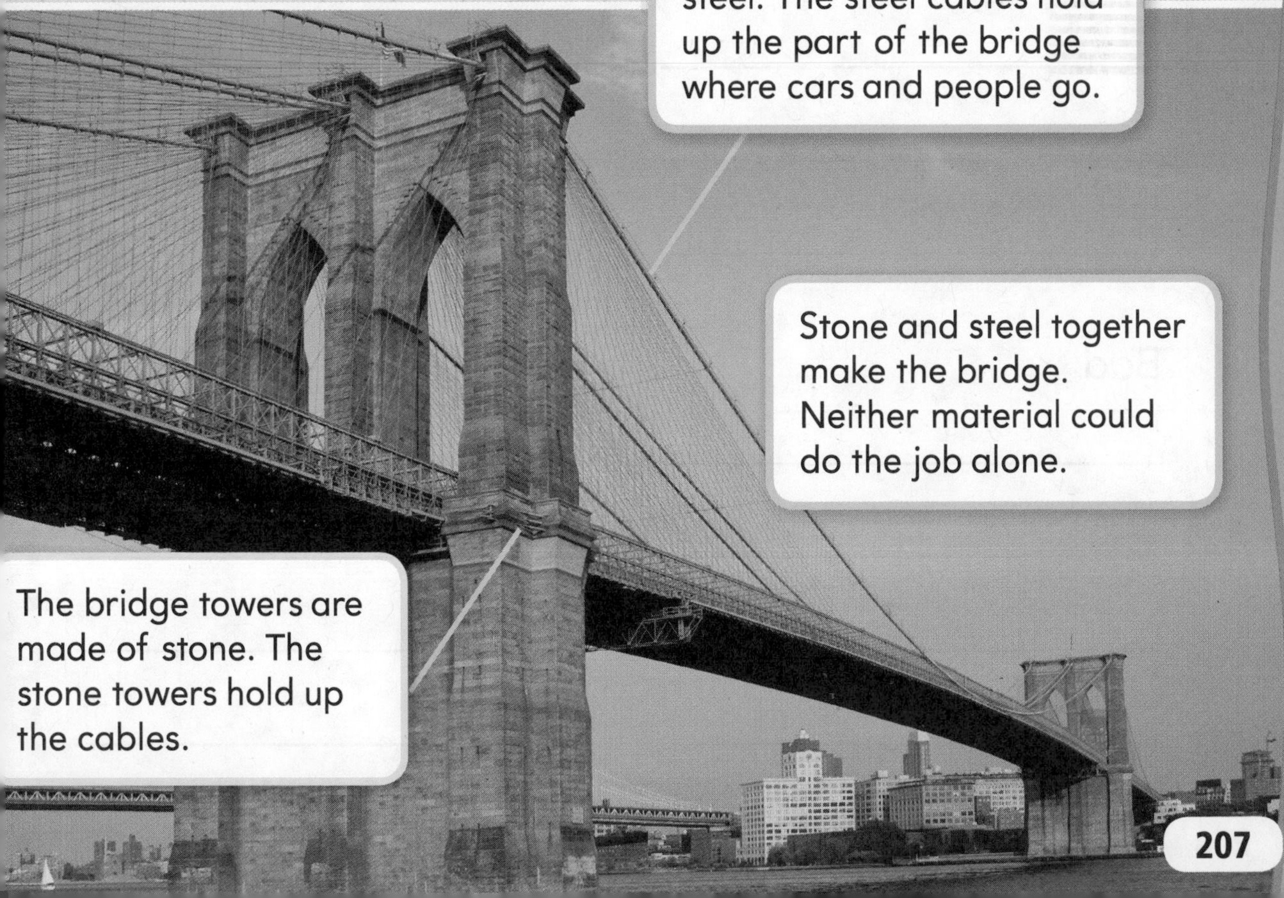

The cables are made of steel. The steel cables hold up the part of the bridge where cars and people go.

Stone and steel together make the bridge. Neither material could do the job alone.

The bridge towers are made of stone. The stone towers hold up the cables.

S.T.E.M. (continued)

Compare Materials

Look at the material used to build each house. Write a possible good thing and bad thing about each material.

WOOD	BRICKS

Good	Good
__________	__________
__________	__________
__________	__________
Bad	Bad
__________	__________
__________	__________
__________	__________
__________	__________

Design It: Combine Materials

Combine materials to make a bridge or tower. What materials will you choose? How will you combine materials so they work together?

▼ The combined materials in a bridge make it strong.

S.T.E.M. (continued)

Design Process Steps: 1 Find a Problem; 2 Plan & Build; 3 Test & Improve; 4 Redesign; 5 Communicate

Make It:

These materials might help you get started.

1. Decide if you will build a bridge or tower.
2. Draw and label your design.
3. Choose your materials. What are their properties? Why did you choose them?
4. Build your bridge or tower.
5. Test your design. Can a box of crayons rest on your bridge for 20 seconds? Does your tower still stand after you gently shake it?
6. Draw and write about your design and results in your Science Notebook.

SC.2.N.1.1 Raise questions ... investigate them in teams ... and generate appropriate explanations based on those explorations. **SC.2.N.1.3 Ask** "how do you know?" in appropriate situations. **SC.2.N.1.4** Explain how ... investigations should yield similar conclusions ... **SC.2.N.1.5** Distinguish between empirical observation ... and ideas or inferences ... **SC.2.P.9.1** Investigate that materials can be altered ... but not all materials respond the same way to any one alteration.

INQUIRY LESSON 2

Name ______________________________

Essential Question

How Can We Change Matter?

EXPLORE

What dissolves in water? Try this investigation to find out.

Before You Begin—Preview the Steps

1. Label one cup **salt**, one cup **sugar**, one cup **sand**, and the last cup **soil**. Fill each of the four plastic cups with warm water.

2. Predict whether the salt will dissolve in the water. Put a spoonful of salt in the cup labeled salt. Stir for 1 minute. Record what you observe.

3. Repeat Step 2 with the sugar, sand, and soil. Which substances dissolved in the water?

4. Repeat the activity. Did you get the same results?

Materials

- 4 clear plastic cups
- marker
- tape or glue
- water
- spoon
- salt
- sugar
- sand
- soil

Set a Purpose

Write what you will do in this investigation.

___

___

___

Make a Prediction

Predict which substances will dissolve in the water.

___

___

___

Think About the Procedure

How do you know when a substance dissolves in water?

___

___

___

Name ______________________

Record Your Data

Write and draw to record your predictions and observations in this chart.

Substance	Prediction	Observation
salt		
sugar		
sand		
soil		

Claims • Evidence • Reasoning

1. Write a claim about whether all substances dissolve in water.

2. What evidence supports your claim?

3. Why does your evidence support your claim?

Ask More Questions

What other questions can you ask about dissolving?

SC.2.N.1.6 Explain how scientists alone or in groups are always investigating new ways to solve problems.

4 Things to Know About Dr. Mei-Yin Chou

1

Dr. Chou was born in Taiwan. She studies physics. Physics is a science that tells about matter and energy.

2

She is a teacher at a university called Georgia Tech.

3

At Georgia Tech, Dr. Chou studies how gases affect solids.

4

She helps girls and women get involved in learning and teaching science.

Word Whiz

▶ Write the words to match the clues.

Taiwan physics gases women Georgia Tech

Across

3 Dr. Chou teaches at this university.

Down

1 Dr. Chou helps them learn about science.

2 This science tells about matter and energy.

4 Dr. Chou studies how these affect solids.

5 Dr. Chou was born in this country.

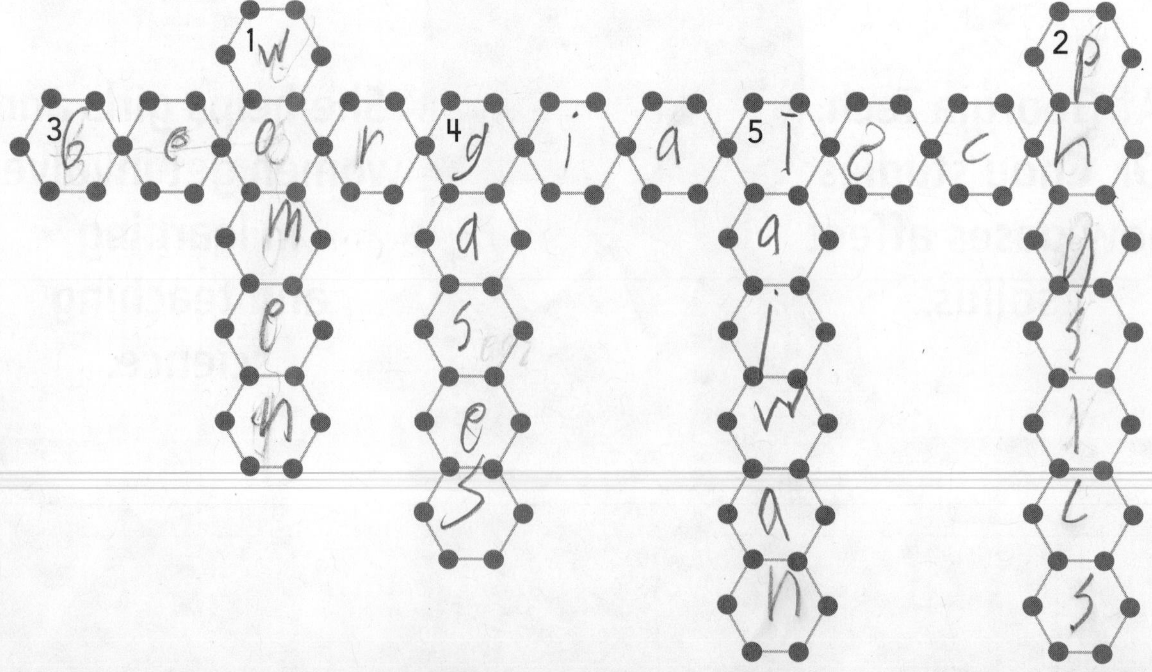

Energy

FLORIDA BIG IDEA 10

Forms of Energy

Jacksonville, Florida skyline at night

I Wonder Why

The city looks very bright at night. Why? *Turn the page to find out.*

Here's Why

Electricity makes the city bright at night. It powers the lights in the buildings.

Essential Questions and Florida Benchmarks

Science Notebook

Before you begin each lesson, write your thoughts about the Essential Question.

SC.2.P.10.1 Discuss that people use electricity or other forms of energy to cook their food, cool or warm their homes, and power their cars.

LESSON 1

Essential Question

How Do We Use Energy?

Engage Your Brain

Find the answer to the question in the lesson.

What makes the wheel move?

____

makes it move.

Active Reading

Lesson Vocabulary

1. Preview the lesson.
2. Write the 5 vocabulary terms here.

______________________ ______________________

______________________ ______________________

____

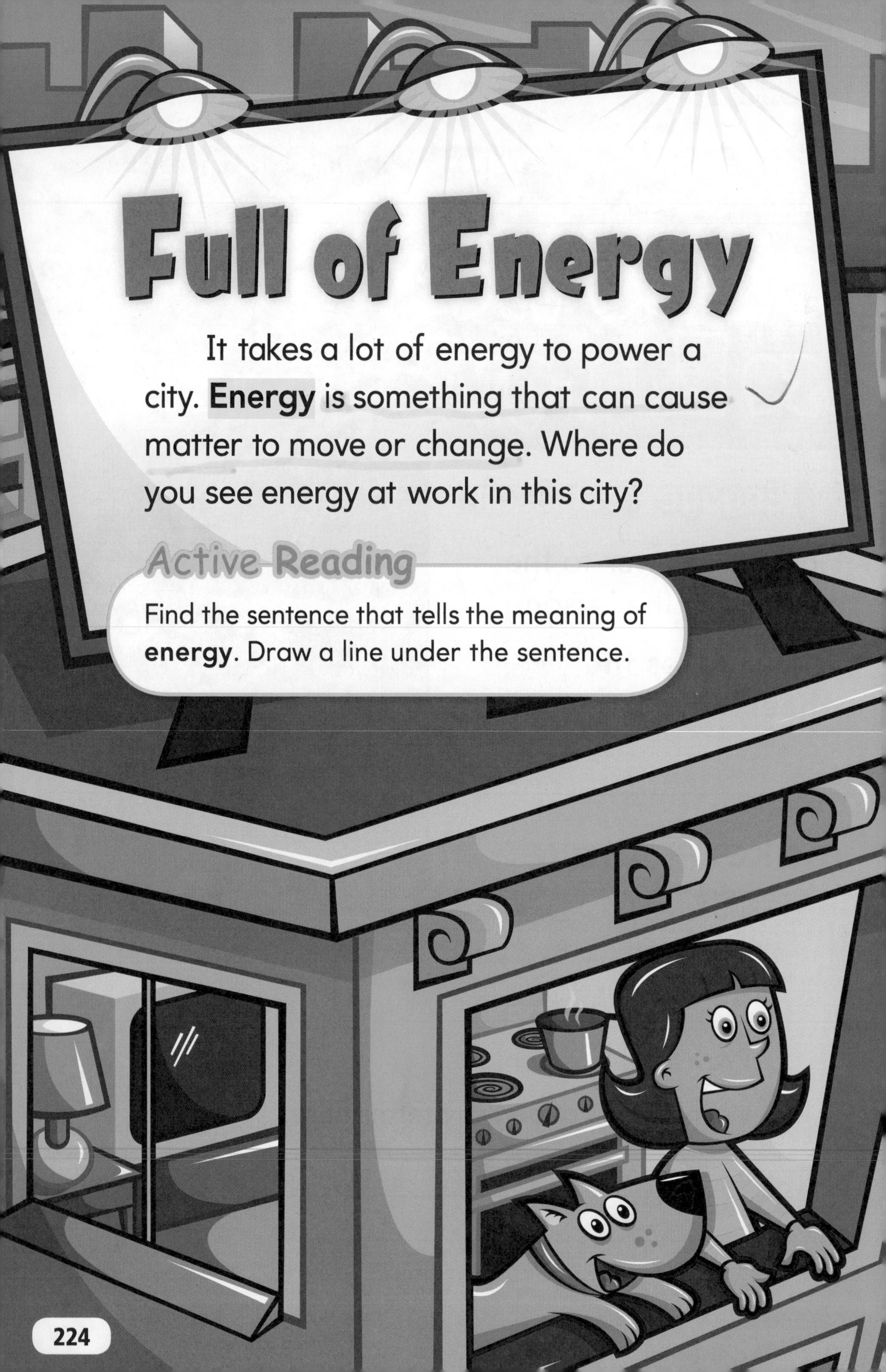

Full of Energy

It takes a lot of energy to power a city. **Energy** is something that can cause matter to move or change. Where do you see energy at work in this city?

Active Reading

Find the sentence that tells the meaning of **energy**. Draw a line under the sentence.

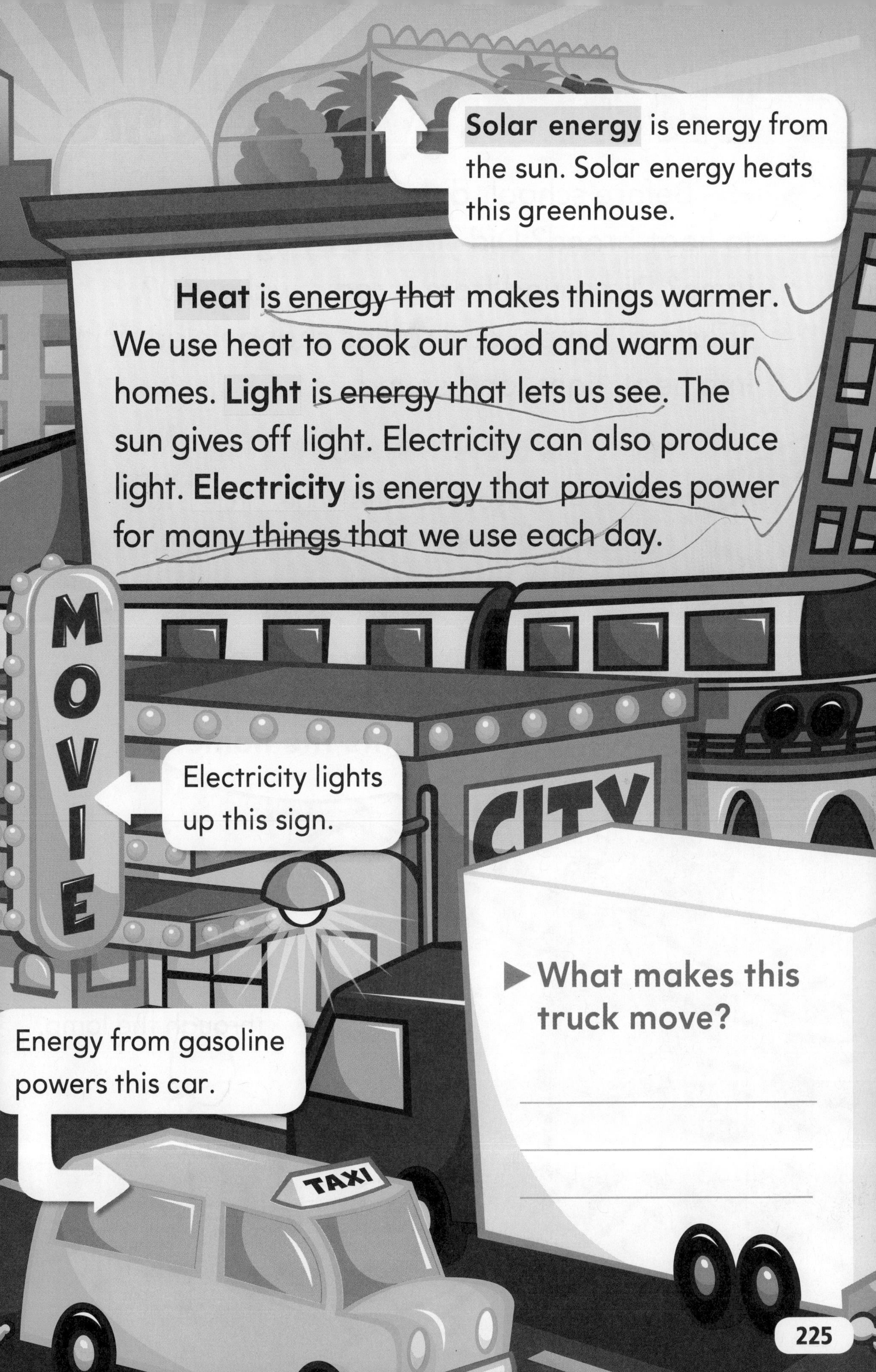

Heat is energy that makes things warmer. We use heat to cook our food and warm our homes. **Light** is energy that lets us see. The sun gives off light. Electricity can also produce light. **Electricity** is energy that provides power for many things that we use each day.

▶ **What makes this truck move?**

____

____

____

Electricity at Home

Before school, did you use a toaster to heat bread? Did you see by light from a lamp? Did sound from a radio wake you? Toasters, lamps, and radios change electricity into heat, light, and sound.

The fan cools the people in the home.
The electric stove cooks food.

Kinds of Energy

Many kinds of energy provide power for the things we use each day. You can see some of these kinds of energy on these pages. People can use most of them to produce electricity.

This dam uses water to produce electricity.

▶ **Name two kinds of energy that you see on these pages.**

Wind turbines collect energy from wind.

Solar panels collect solar energy.

Do the Math

Solve a Problem

Read the word problem. Answer the question.

There are 2 solar panels on each house. How many solar panels are there on 4 houses?

____

Sum It Up »

1 Label It!

Look at the pictures. Complete the labels to tell why you use each thing.

to cool **people** **to** cook **food** **to** light **a desk**

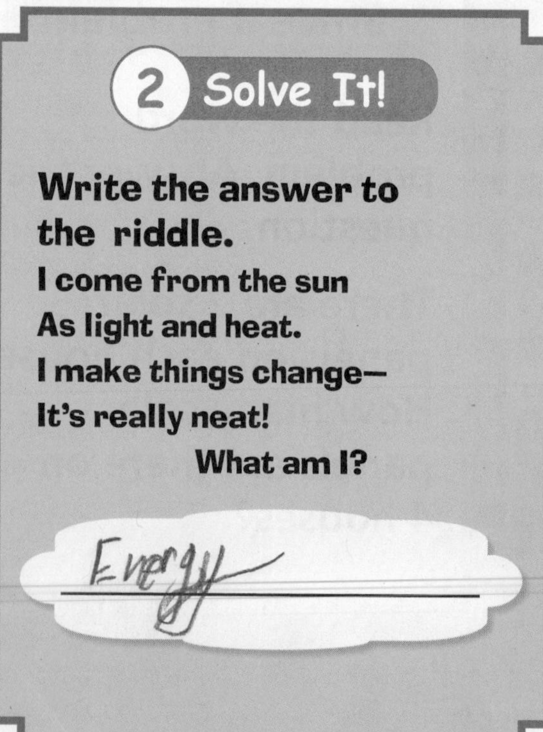

2 Solve It!

Write the answer to the riddle.

I come from the sun
As light and heat.
I make things change—
It's really neat!
What am I?

Energy

3 Draw It!

Draw a way that you use electricity.

SC.2.N.1.1 Raise questions ... investigate them in teams ... and generate appropriate explanations based on those explorations. SC.2.P.10.1 Discuss that people use electricity or other forms of energy ....

INQUIRY LESSON 2

Name ____________________

Essential Question

How Does the Sun Warm Our Homes?

Materials

cardboard box
scissors
plastic wrap
tape
2 thermometers

EXPLORE

How does solar energy warm our homes? Make a model to find out.

Before You Begin—Preview the Steps

1. Use the box and the plastic wrap to make a model house.
   Caution! Be careful when using scissors.

2. Tape one thermometer to a window inside the house. Record the temperatures on both thermometers.

3. Put the house in a sunny spot. Lay the other thermometer next to the house. Wait 1 hour. Record both temperatures again. Compare the numbers.

Set a Purpose

Explain what you will learn from this activity.

____

____

State Your Hypothesis

Write your hypothesis, or statement that you will test.

____

____

____

Think About the Procedure

Why do you need to measure the temperature both outside the model and inside the model?

____

____

____

Name ___________________________

Record Your Data

Record your observations in this chart.

Place	Temperature at Start	Temperature After 1 Hour
Inside the Model		
Outside the Model		

Show your data in a bar graph.

Claims • Evidence • Reasoning

1. Write a claim about how the sun warms our homes.

2. What evidence supports your claim?

3. Why does your evidence support your claim?

Ask More Questions

What other questions can you ask about how the sun warms our homes?

4 Things to Know About Dr. Lawnie Taylor

1. Dr. Taylor studied physics. Physics is a science that tells about matter and energy.

2. He worked for the U.S. Department of Energy for many years.

3. He studied ways to use the sun's energy to heat homes and produce electricity.

4. Dr. Taylor also studied ways to use the sun's energy to make machines run.

PEOPLE IN SCIENCE

Let the Sun Shine!

Dr. Taylor studied solar energy. Now you can, too!

▶ **Write the number of each description next to the correct picture.**

1. **Solar panels on a house collect the sun's energy to produce electricity or heat water.**
2. **A solar farm can change the sun's energy into electricity for many people to use.**
3. **A solar car uses the sun's energy to make it run.**

▶ **How have you seen solar energy used?**

____

____

SC.2.N.1.6 Explain how scientists alone or in groups are always investigating new ways to solve problems. SC.2.P.10.1 Discuss that people use electricity or other forms of energy to cook their food, cool or warm their homes, and power their cars.

S.T.E.M.

ENGINEERING & TECHNOLOGY

Changing Cars

Building a Better Car

Most cars run on gas. These cars make air pollution. Engineers are making new cars that are better for the air.

gas car

A hybrid car runs on gas and electricity. It makes less pollution than a car that runs only on gas.

An electric car runs on electricity. It does not make any pollution at all!

hybrid car

electric car

Electric cars run for only a short time. Engineers are working on this problem.

S.T.E.M. (continued)

Which Car Is Best?

Read the sentences below.
Then answer the questions.

You want to take a short car trip. You do not want to make any pollution. Which car would you choose to take your trip? Why?

____

____

____

____

____

____

ENGINEERING
DESIGN CHALLENGE

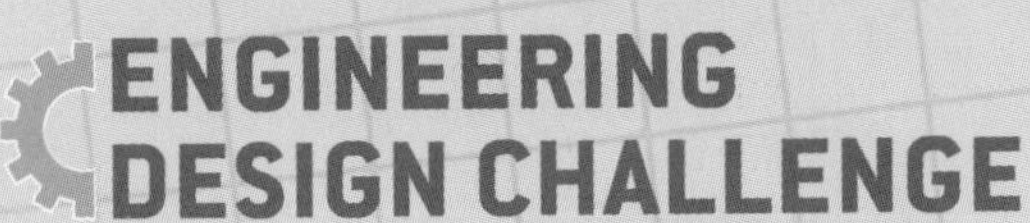

Solve It:

Use Fewer Cars

Cars can pollute the air with harmful fumes. This is a problem. Engineers try to solve problems like air pollution. You can think of ideas, too. Use the questions in the *What to Do* section to help you.

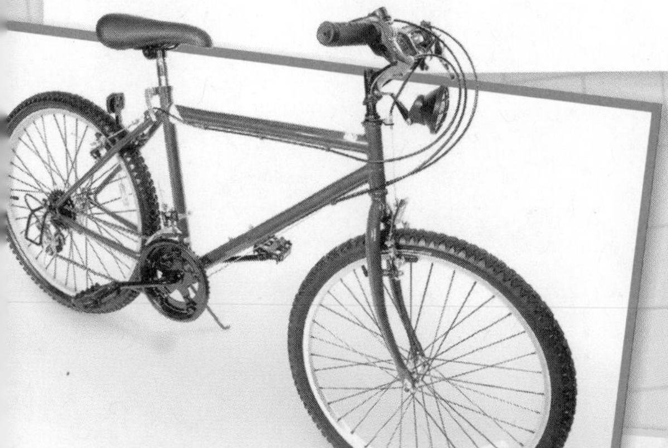

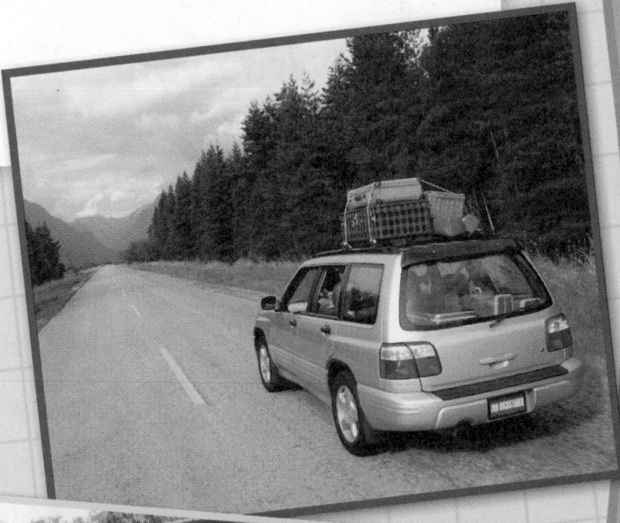

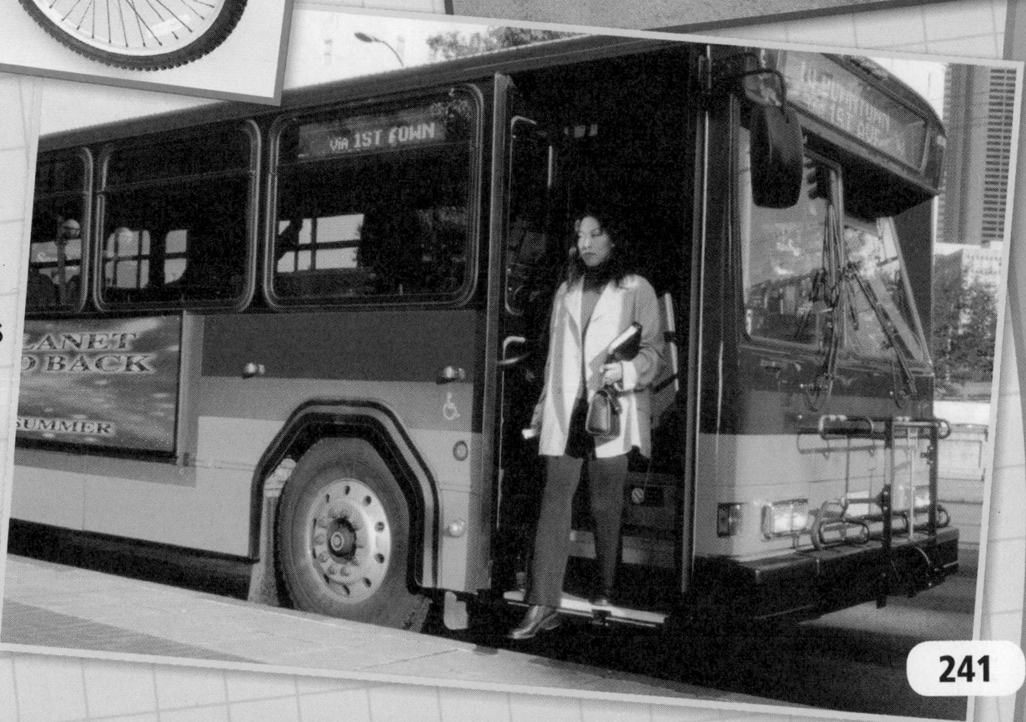

How can riding a bike or a bus help reduce air pollution?

S.T.E.M. (continued)

What to Do:

1. What are some reasons to use fewer cars? How can people use fewer cars?
2. Use your answers to think of ways you can help prevent air pollution.
3. Write your ideas in your Science Notebook.

Forces and Motion

Properties of Matter

Forces and Changes in Motion

speed boat in Florida

I Wonder Why

This speed boat moves faster over the water than other boats. Why? *Turn the page to find out.*

Here's Why

Applying more force to an object will cause it to move faster.

Essential Questions and Florida Benchmarks

Before you begin each lesson, write your thoughts about the Essential Question.

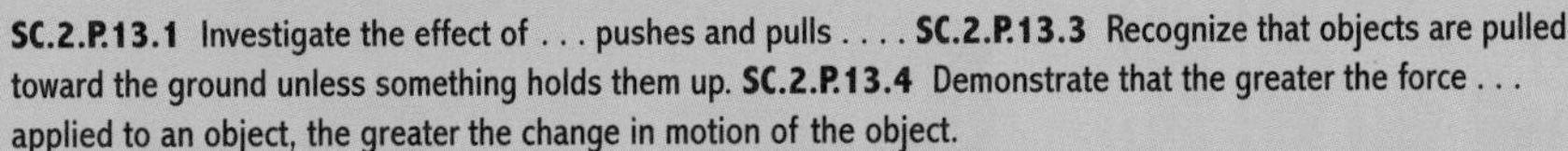

SC.2.P.13.1 Investigate the effect of . . . pushes and pulls . . . . **SC.2.P.13.3** Recognize that objects are pulled toward the ground unless something holds them up. **SC.2.P.13.4** Demonstrate that the greater the force . . . applied to an object, the greater the change in motion of the object.

Essential Question

What Are Forces?

Engage Your Brain

Find the answer to the question in the lesson.

The chair is holding up the circus star. What force is pulling down on him?

__________ is pulling down on him.

Active Reading

Lesson Vocabulary

1. Preview the lesson.
2. Write the 5 vocabulary terms here.

__________ __________

__________ __________

____

In Full Force

This rope is moving round and round. It is in motion. **Motion** means movement. Something that is moving is in motion.

A juggler makes rings move in different ways. The juggler uses forces to change their motion. A **force** is a push or a pull. How do you use forces to change motion?

Active Reading

Find the sentence that tells the meaning of **force**. Draw a line under the sentence.

A **push** is a force that moves something away from you. A **pull** is a force that moves something toward you.

The juggler uses pushes and pulls to change how the rings move.

▶ **Draw a push or a pull.**

Up to Speed

How do acrobats fly through the air? They use forces to change their speed and direction. **Speed** is how fast something moves. A small force changes an object's speed and direction a little. A large force can change them a lot.

The acrobats are using forces to change direction.

▶ **What happens to the speed of the cart if you give it a big push?**

it will go faster

The harder the acrobats push and pull, the faster they go.

Down to Earth

If you drop a ball, it falls. Why? The answer is gravity. **Gravity** is a force that pulls all things toward the center of Earth. Things fall to the ground unless something holds them up.

Active Reading

A detail is a fact about a main idea. Draw one line under a detail about gravity. Draw an arrow to the main idea it tells about.

▶ **Put an X on the object holding this man up.**

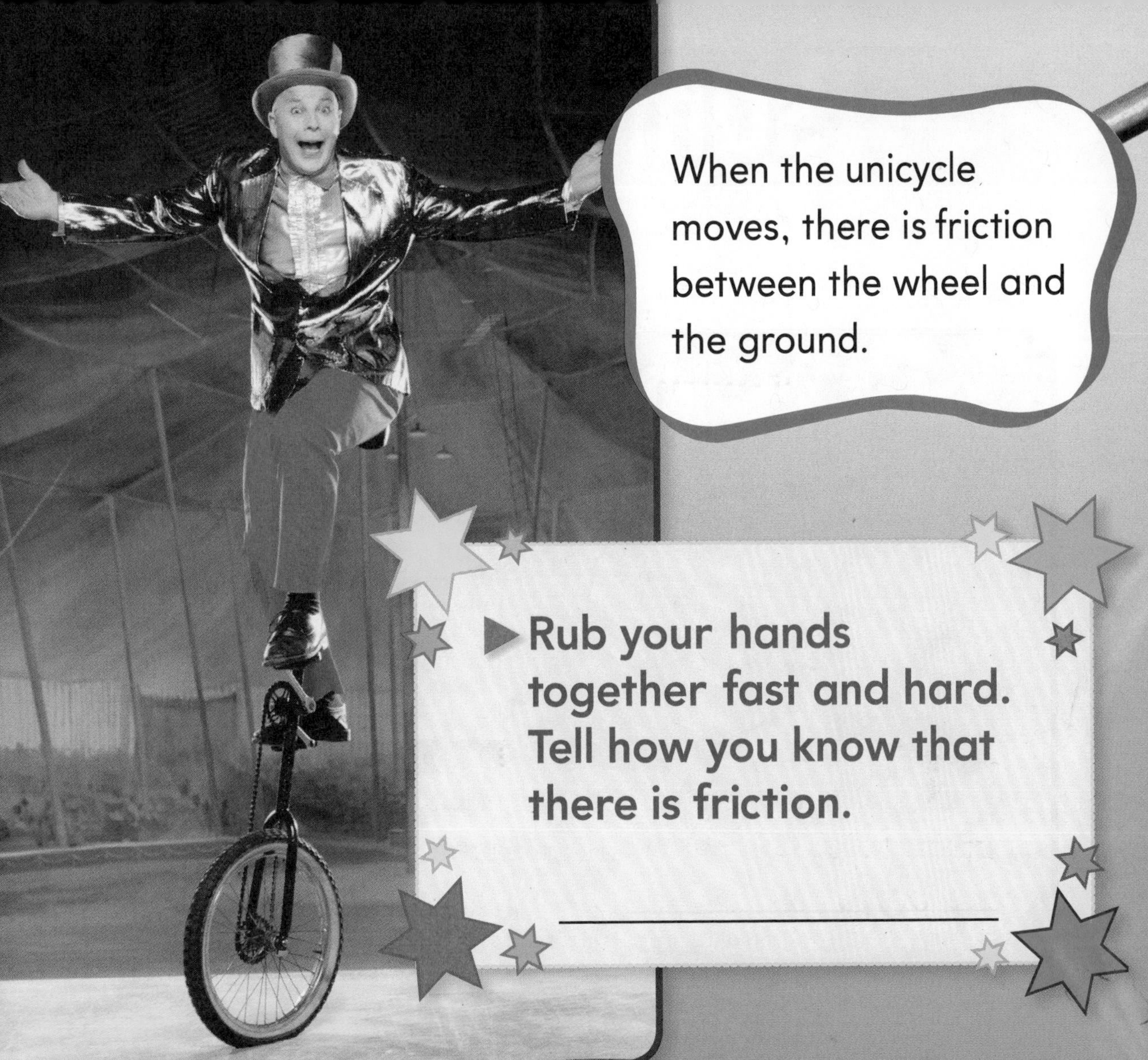

▶ Rub your hands together fast and hard. Tell how you know that there is friction.

____

Slow Down!

Think about riding your bike. You might not know it, but friction is at work between the tires and the road. **Friction** is a force that slows or stops things that are touching. Friction also causes objects to get warmer when they rub together. How does friction affect the bike?

Sum It Up »

1 Label It!

Write push or pull to label each picture.

2 Solve It!

Write the answer to the riddle.

You can't see me,
but I am a force.
I pull things to Earth—
a pen, an egg, or
even a horse!
What am I?

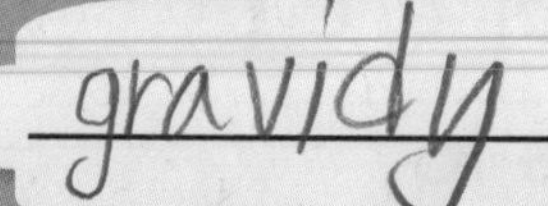

3 Circle It!

Circle the answer.

Jay pushes a box with a little force. Then he pushes it with a lot more force. How will he change the box's speed?

The box goes ______ faster.

much **a little**

LESSON 1

Name ____________________

Vocabulary Review

Write a word from the box for each definition.

1. a force that slows or stops things that are touching f r i c t i o n (1: f, 4: c)

2. a force that pulls things toward the center of Earth g r a v i d y (3: r)

3. tells how fast something moves s p e e d (5: e)

4. when something moves m o t i o n (2: o)

Solve the riddle. Write the circled letters in order on the lines below.

I am a push or pull. What am I?

f o r c e

1 2 3 4 5

Apply Concepts

Write a cause or effect in each row to complete the chart.

Forces

Cause	Effect
gravity	pulls things to the center of the earth
pull	Something moves closer to you.
friction	Things slow down or stop and get warmer.
push	moves things away
force	Things may change speed or direction.

Family Members: *See ScienceSaurus®* for more information about forces.

SC.2.N.1.1 Raise questions ... investigate them in teams ... and generate appropriate explanations based on those explorations. SC.2.N.1.3 Ask "how do you know?" in appropriate situations ... SC.2.N.1.5 Distinguish between empirical observation ... and ideas or inferences ... SC.2.P.13.1 Investigate the effect of ... pushes and pulls ... SC.2.P.13.4 Demonstrate that the greater the force ... applied to an object, the greater the change in motion of the object.

Name ________________________________

Essential Question

How Do Forces Make Objects Move?

Materials

- yardstick
- masking tape
- marker
- piece of paper
- straw
- stopwatch

EXPLORE

What happens to an object's speed if the force on the object increases? Let's investigate to find out.

Before You Begin—Preview the Steps

1. Use masking tape to mark a Start and a Finish line 3 feet apart on the floor. Make a small paper ball.
2. Use the straw to gently blow the ball from the Start to the Finish line. Have a partner time how long it takes. Record the time.
3. Repeat Step 2. But this time, blow the paper ball hard. What can you infer about the speed of the paper ball in each trial?

Set a Purpose

Write what you want to find out.

___

___

State Your Hypothesis

Write your hypothesis, or statement that you will test.

___

___

Think About the Procedure

How does measuring time tell you about speed?

___

___

___

___

Name ______________________

Record Your Data

Record your observations in this chart.

Force	Amount of Time
Less Force	
More Force	

Show your data in a bar graph.

Claims • Evidence • Reasoning

1. Write a claim about how force affects the speed of an object.

____

____

2. What evidence supports your claim?

____

____

3. Why does your evidence support your claim?

____

____

____

Ask More Questions

What other questions can you ask about how force changes the motion of objects?

____

____

____

____

SC.2.P.8.1 Observe and measure objects in terms of their properties, including . . . . attraction and repulsion of magnets. SC.2.P.13.2 Demonstrate that magnets can be used to make some things move without touching them.

LESSON 3

Essential Question

What Are Magnets?

Engage Your Brain

Find the answer to the question in the lesson.

What objects are making this smiley face?

____

Active Reading

Lesson Vocabulary

1. Preview the lesson.
2. Write the 4 vocabulary terms here.

_______________ _______________

_______________ _______________

Magnetic Pull

A **magnet** is an object that can pull things made of iron and steel. A magnet can push or pull other magnets.

A magnet has two poles. A **pole** is a place on a magnet where the pull is the greatest. One pole is the north-seeking, or **N**, pole. The other pole is the south-seeking, or **S**, pole.

Active Reading

Find the sentence that tells the meaning of **pole**. Draw a line under the sentence.

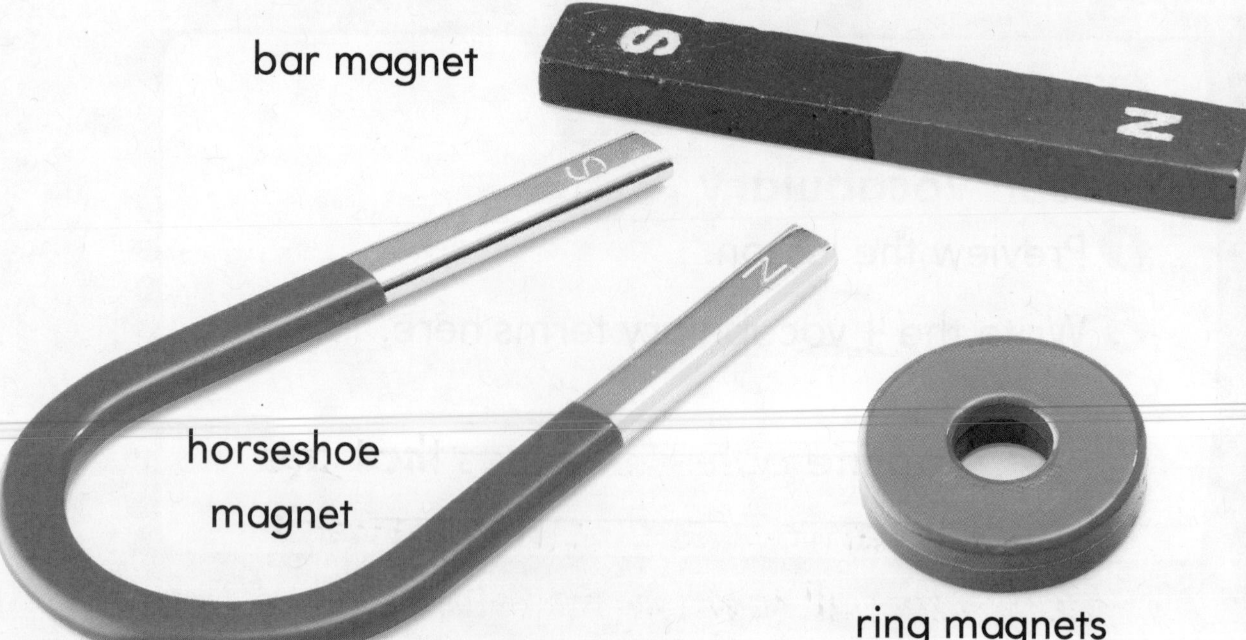

bar magnet

horseshoe magnet

ring magnets

Like poles, or poles that are the same, repel each other. **Repel** means to push away from something.

▶ **Draw two bar magnets to show another way they can repel.**

Opposite poles, or poles that are different, attract each other. **Attract** means to pull toward something.

ATTRACT ATTENTION

A steel paper clip is attracted to a magnet. A rubber band is not. Magnets attract some things but not others. Look at these boxes. Which things are attracted to a magnet? Which things are not?

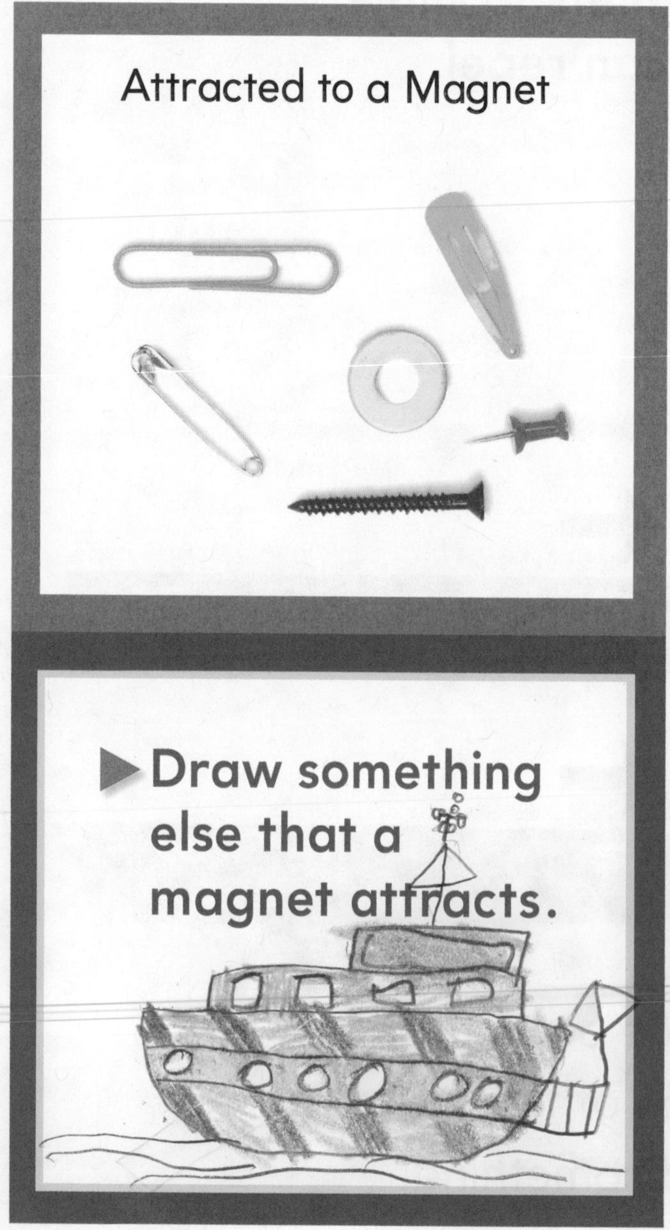

Look at the way the magnet pulls the paper clips right through the hand! A magnet does not have to touch an object to move it. This is possible because of its magnetic field. This is the area around a magnet where the magnetic force is felt.

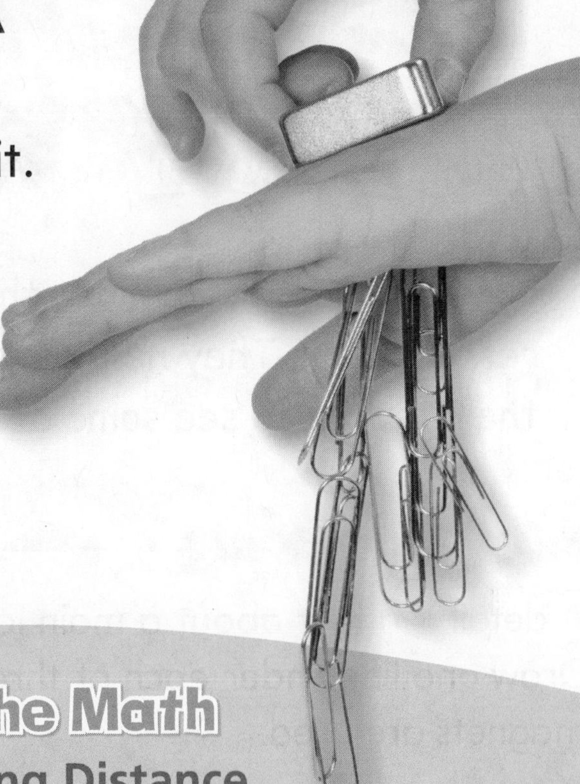

Do the Math

Measuring Distance

How far from a paper clip must a magnet be before it does not attract it? Use a ruler to measure.

Distance	Did the magnet attract the paper clip?
½ inch	
1 inch	
1½ inches	
2 inches	

How far from the magnet can you observe the magnetic field? How do you know?

____

____

MAGNETS EVERYWHERE

Magnets do much more than stick papers to the refrigerator. They help us in amazing ways! Look at the pictures to see some of the things magnets can do.

Active Reading

A detail is a fact about a main idea. Reread the captions. Draw one line under each of three details about how magnets are used.

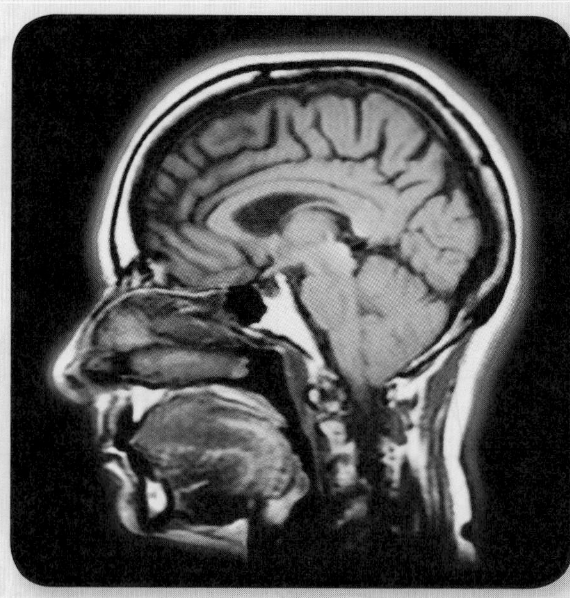

Magnets in MRI machines help make pictures of the inside of our bodies.

Huge magnets help sort items made of iron and steel before they are recycled.

▶ **Draw a way you use magnets.**

A Maglev train uses magnets to lift and move the train forward. One train has gone 361 miles per hour!

Sum It Up »

1 Circle It!

Circle the objects a magnet attracts.

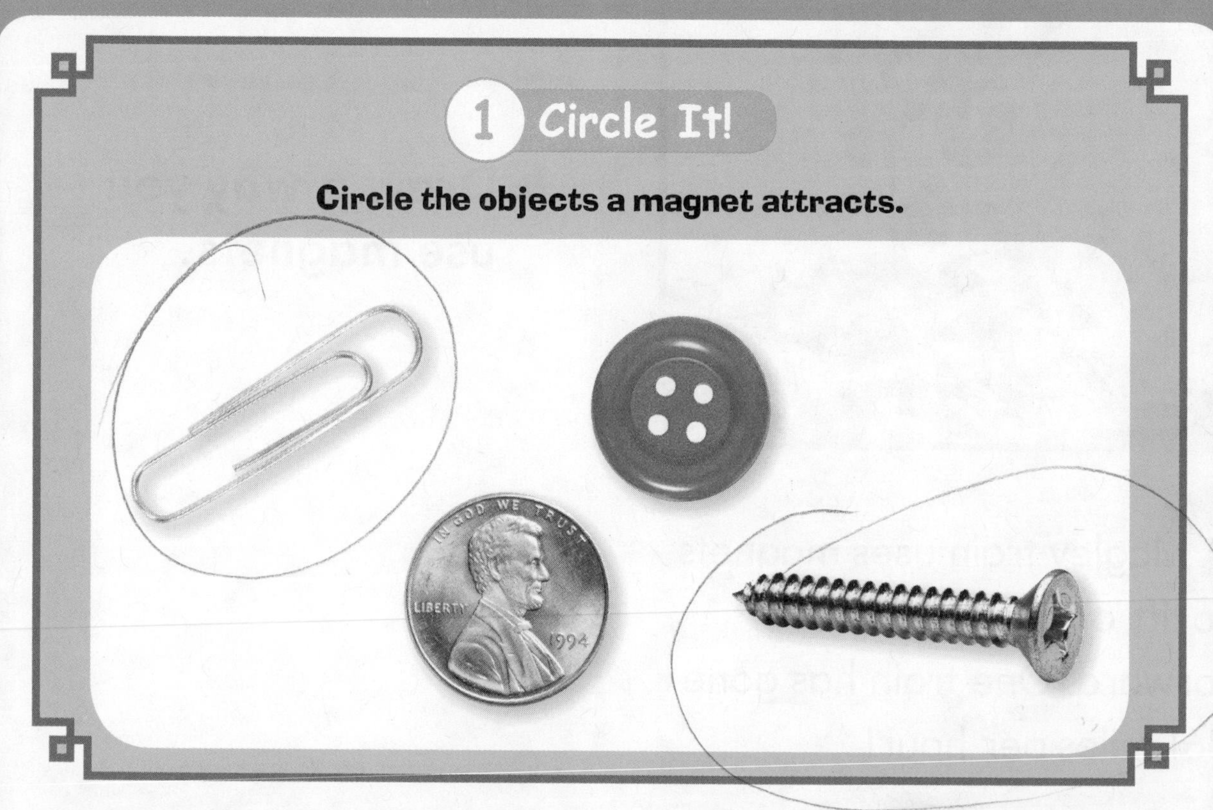

2 Answer It!

Circle true or false to describe the statement.

A magnet must touch an object to attract it.

true false

3 Draw It!

Draw a way you can use a magnet.

Brain Check

LESSON 3

Name ___

Vocabulary Review

Write a word from the word bank on each line to complete the friendly letter.

magnets	poles	attract	repel

Dear Uncle Herbie,

Thanks for the science kit! I like the magnets the best. They make some objects move without touching them. I used the big magnet to attract an iron nail.

Each magnet has two places where the pull is the strongest. These places are called poles. When two poles that are the same are pointed toward each other, they repel. They push apart really hard.

Your niece,

Olivia

Apply Concepts

Complete this graphic organizer. Write an important detail about magnets in each box.

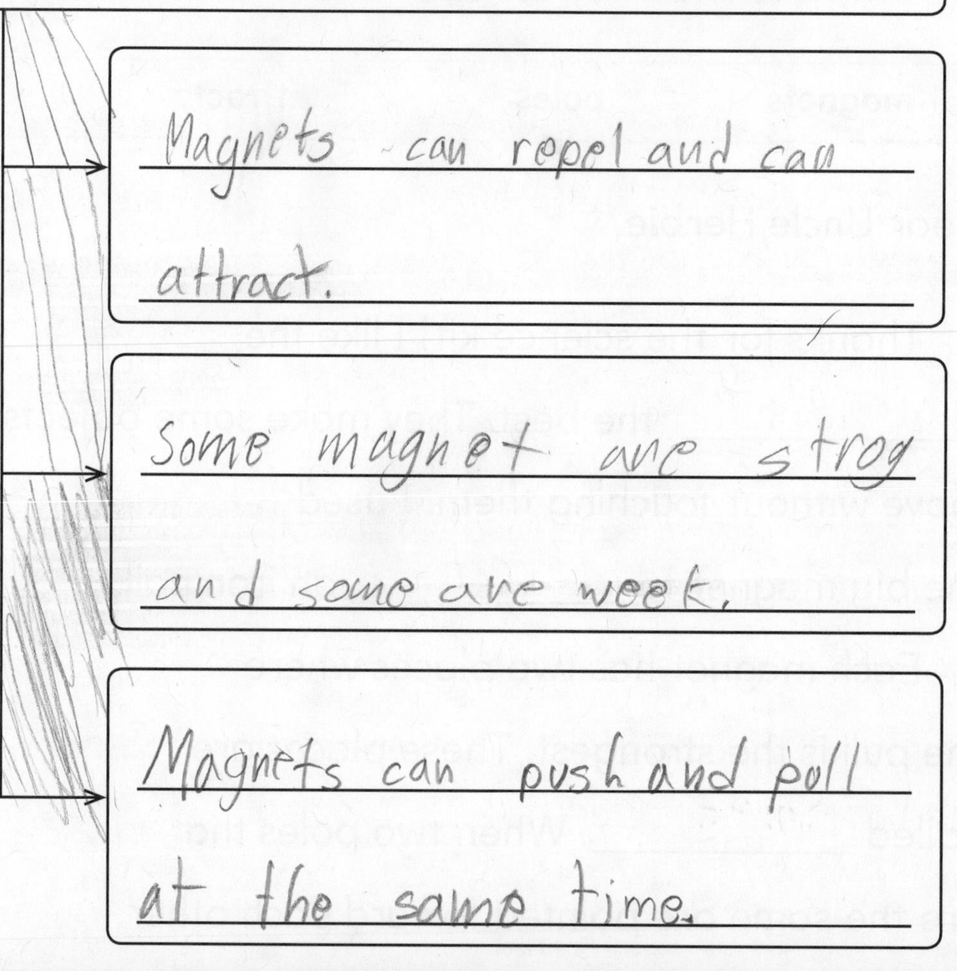

Family Members: Ask your child to tell you about magnets. Ask him or her to point out how magnets work and how they are used in everyday life.

SC.2.N.1.1 Raise questions ..., investigate them in teams ..., and generate appropriate explanations based on those explorations. SC.2.N.1.2 Compare the observations made ... using the same tools. SC.2.N.1.3 Ask "how do you know?" in appropriate situations ... SC.2.P.8.1 Observe and measure objects in terms of their properties, including ... attraction and repulsion of magnets. SC.2.P.1.3.2 Demonstrate that magnets can be used to make some things move without touching them.

Name ___________________________

ssential Question

How Strong Is a Magnet?

Materials

- string
- large paper clip
- tape
- magnet
- piece of paper
- other classroom objects

XPLORE

Can a magnet attract a paper clip through different objects? Let's investigate to find out.

Before You Begin—Preview the Steps

1. Tie some string around a paper clip. Tape the string to a table. Let the paper clip hang over the end of the table.

2. Put a piece of paper in between the paper clip and the magnet. Move the magnet back and forth. Record what happens.

3. Repeat Step 2 with other classroom objects. What did you observe? Compare your results with those of classmates.

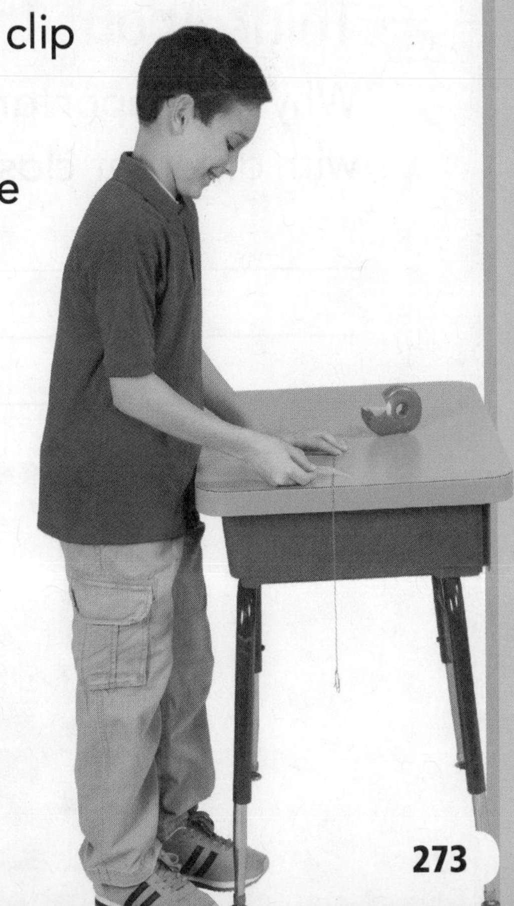

Set a Purpose

Write what you want to find out.

State Your Hypothesis

Write your hypothesis, or the statement that you will test.

Think About the Procedure

Why is it important to test the strength of the magnet with different classroom objects?

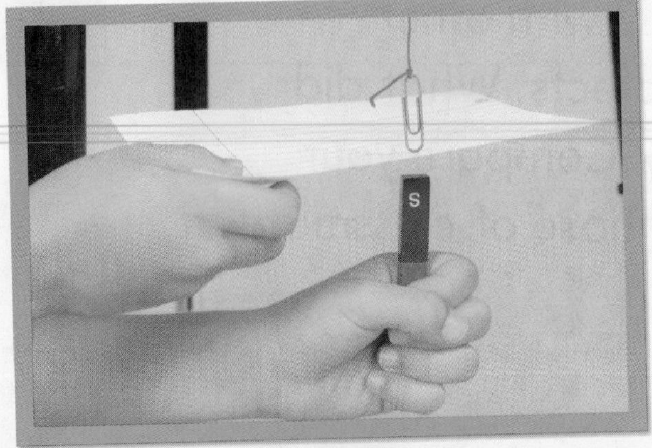

Name ______________________________

Record Your Data

Record your observations in this chart. Write the names of the three objects you tested. Circle attracts or does not attract based on your results.

Object	Attracts/Does Not Attract	
Object 1: piece of paper	attracts	does not attract
Object 2:	attracts	does not attract
Object 3:	attracts	does not attract
Object 4:	attracts	does not attract

Claims • Evidence • Reasoning

1. Write a claim about how putting something between the magnet and the paper clip affects the strength of the magnet.

2. What evidence supports your claim?

3. Why does your evidence support your claim?

Ask More Questions

What other questions can you ask about magnets?

SC.2.N.1.1 Raise questions ... and generate appropriate explanations based on those explorations. SC.2.N.1.2 Compare the observations made ... SC.2.N.1.3 Ask "how do you know?" in appropriate situations ... SC.2.P.8.1 Observe and measure objects in terms of their properties, including ... attraction and repulsion of magnets. SC.2.P.13.2 Demonstrate that magnets can be used to make some things move without touching them.

S.T.E.M.

ENGINEERING & TECHNOLOGY

Magnets All Around

Everyday Magnets

Magnets are used in many everyday things.

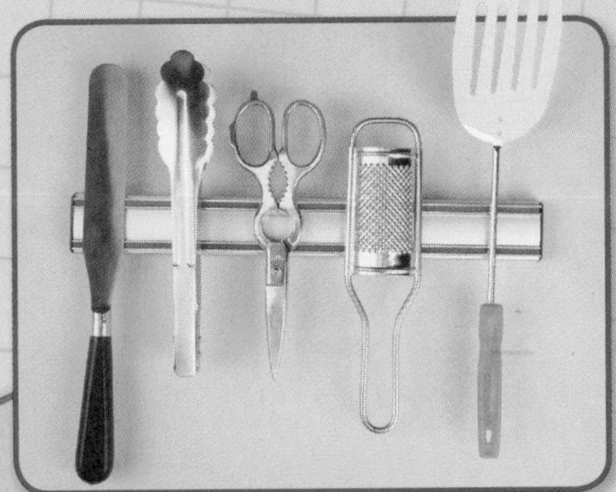

A magnet keeps these kitchen tools in order.

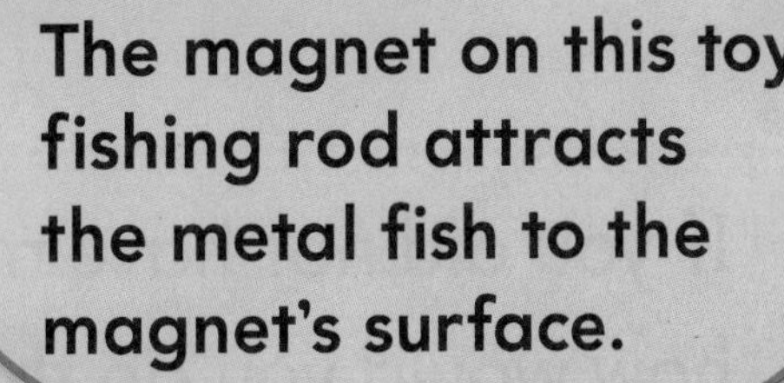

The magnet on this toy fishing rod attracts the metal fish to the magnet's surface.

Magnets help keep the refrigerator door closed. They also attach the magnetic letters to the door.

S.T.E.M. (continued)

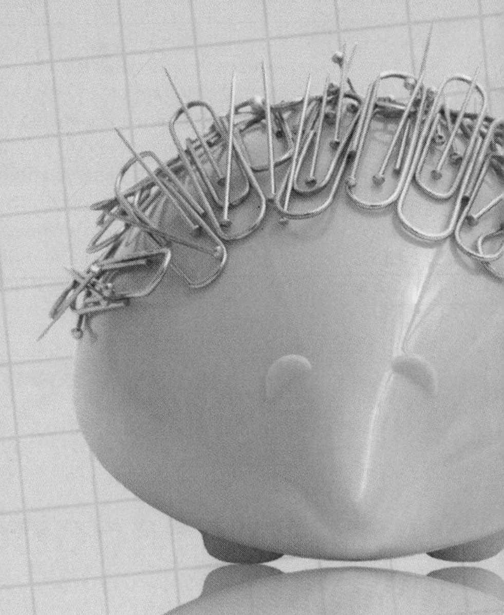

Classroom Magnets

Draw two ways that magnets are used in your classroom.

If you did not have magnets in your classroom, how would you do the things that you drew?

____

____

____

ENGINEERING DESIGN CHALLENGE

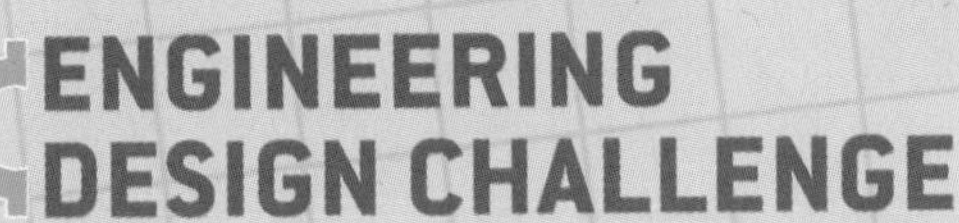

Design It: Use Magnets

Magnets can keep doors open or closed. They are part of many games and toys. How can you use magnets? Design a tool or game for your classroom that includes at least one magnet.

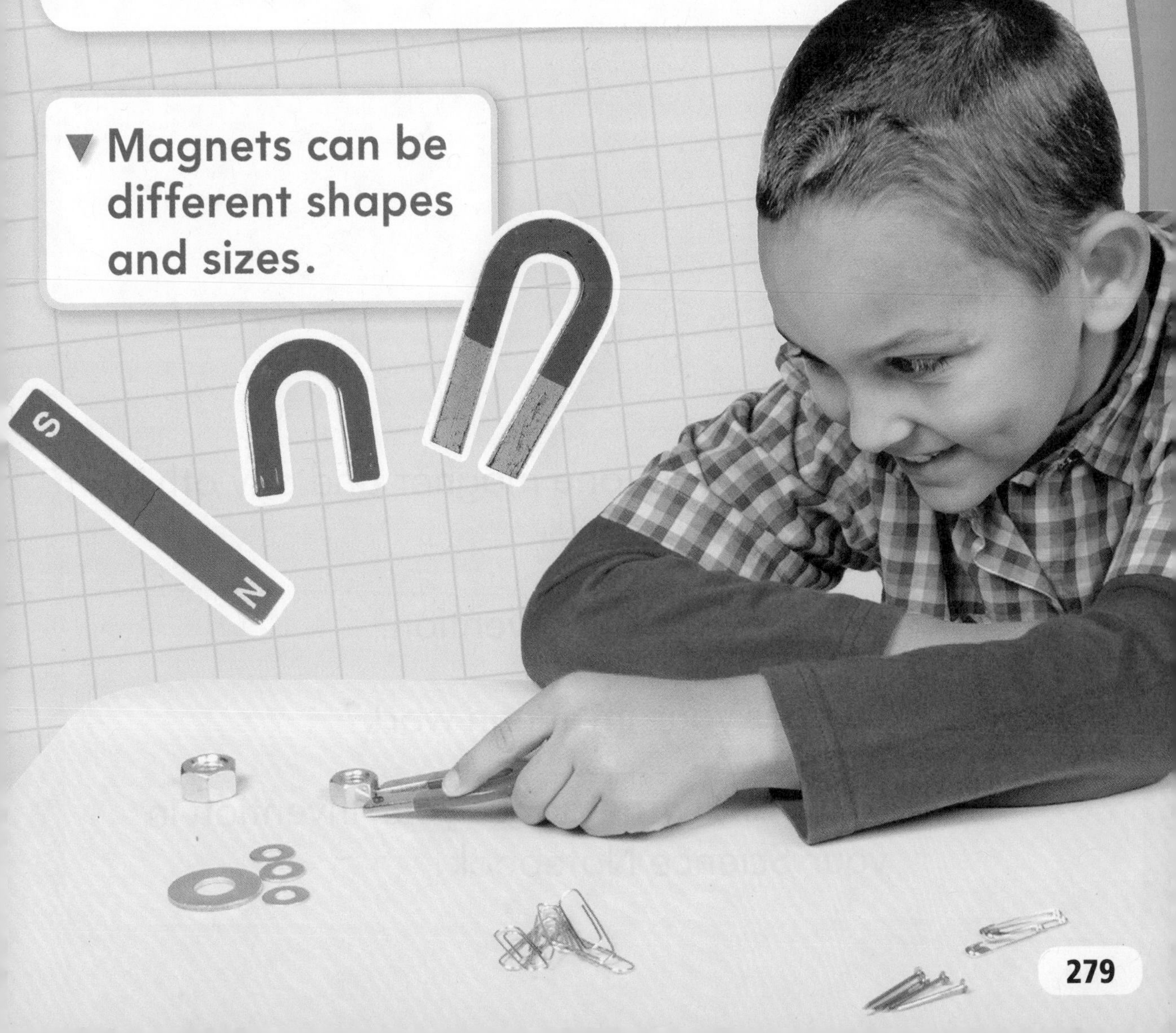

▼ Magnets can be different shapes and sizes.

S.T.E.M. (continued)

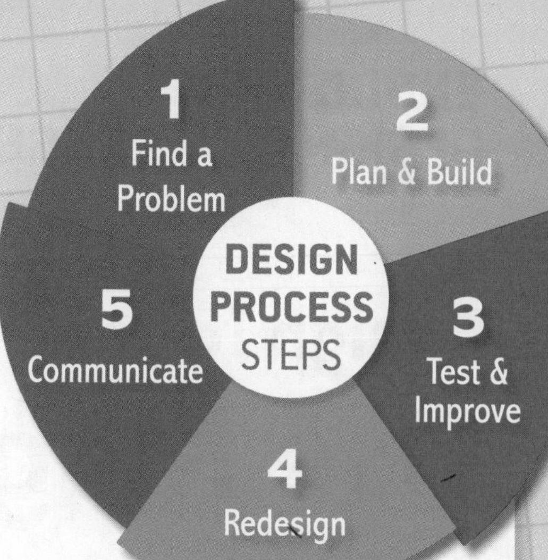

What to Do:

1. Draw your design.

2. Gather at least one magnet and any other materials you need.

3. Build and test your invention.

4. How does your invention work?

5. Draw and write about your invention in your Science Notebook.

The Human Body

Organization and Development of Living Organisms

skateboarding in Florida

I Wonder Why

It is important to wear safety gear when exercising. Why?
Turn the page to find out.

Here's Why

Safety gear protects your muscles, bones, and other body parts.

Essential Questions and Florida Benchmarks

Science Notebook

Before you begin each lesson, write your thoughts about the Essential Question.

Essential Question

What Makes Up the Human Body?

Engage Your Brain

Find the answer to the riddle in the lesson.

Your hand has about 27 of these. They help your hand move.

They are ________.

Active Reading

Lesson Vocabulary

1. Preview the lesson.
2. Write the 6 vocabulary terms here.

________ ________

________ ________

________ ________

Your Body

Starring Your Brain

brain

Your body is amazing! It has many parts. The parts work together. They help keep you alive.

Your **brain** is one important body part. Your brain tells your other body parts what to do. Your brain lets you think, remember, and feel.

Active Reading

Find the sentences that tell what your brain does. Draw a line under the sentences.

Your Stomach

When you swallow, food moves from your mouth through a tube called the esophagus. Then the food moves into your stomach.

Your **stomach** helps digest, or break down, food. Your body uses the nutrients in the food. Then you can run, play, and think.

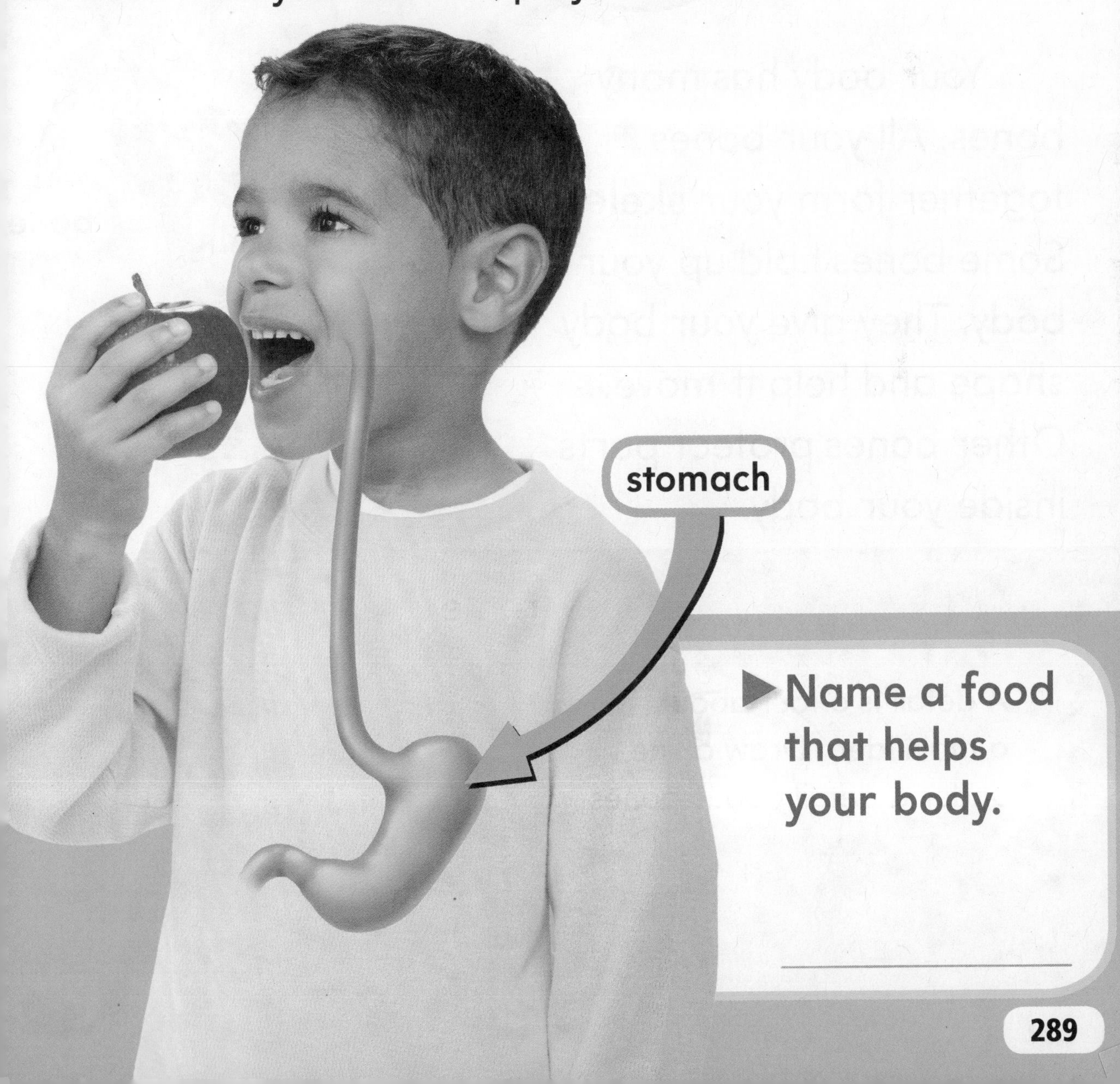

▶ **Name a food that helps your body.**

____

Your Skeleton and Muscles

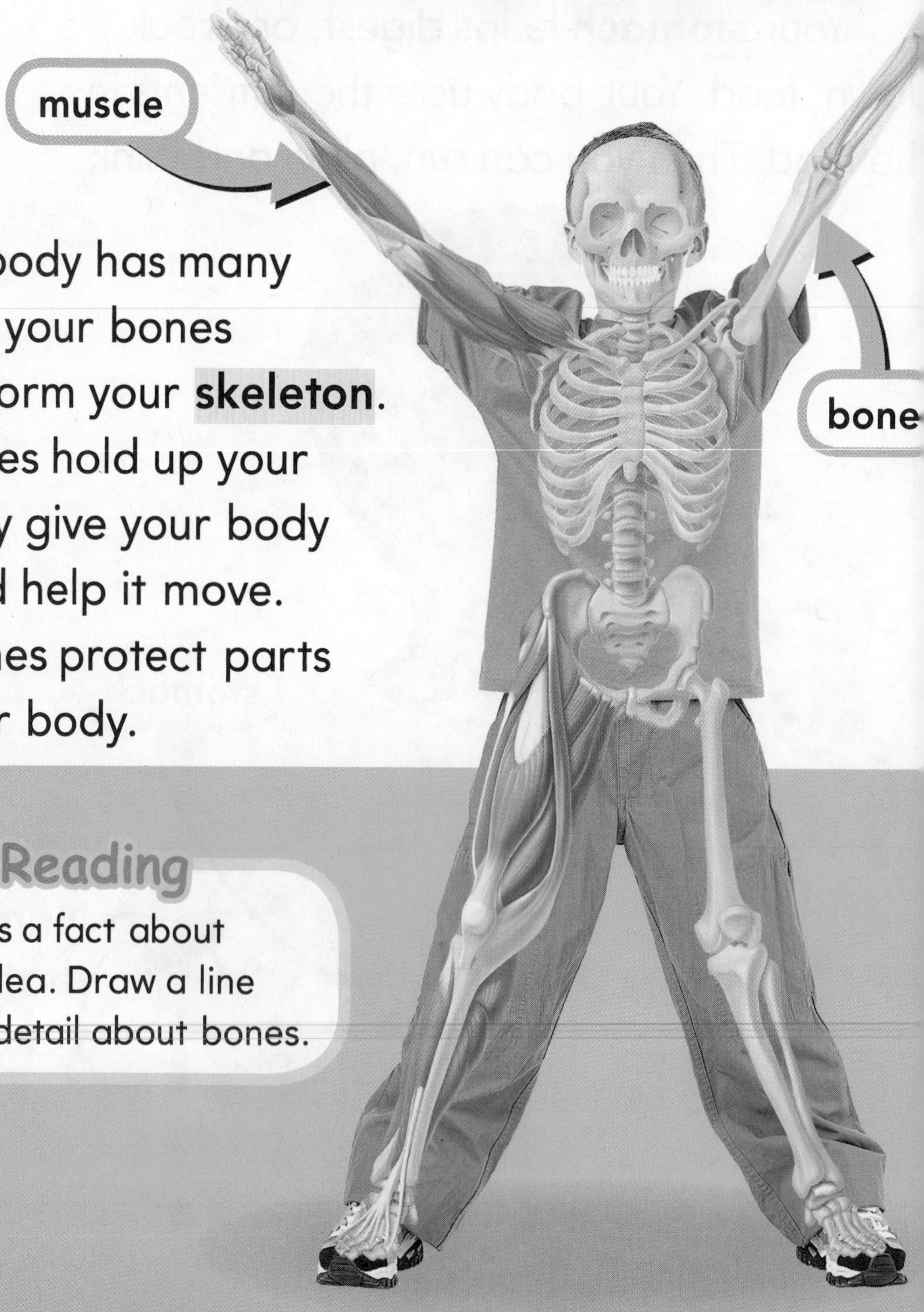

muscle

bone

Your body has many bones. All your bones together form your **skeleton**. Some bones hold up your body. They give your body shape and help it move. Other bones protect parts inside your body.

Active Reading

A detail is a fact about a main idea. Draw a line under a detail about bones.

You have **muscles** all over your ody. Some muscles pull on your ones to move them. Other muscles ove things like nutrients and oxygen rough your body.

▶ **How do your bones and muscles work together?**

____

____

Your Lungs

Your lungs ar
in your chest

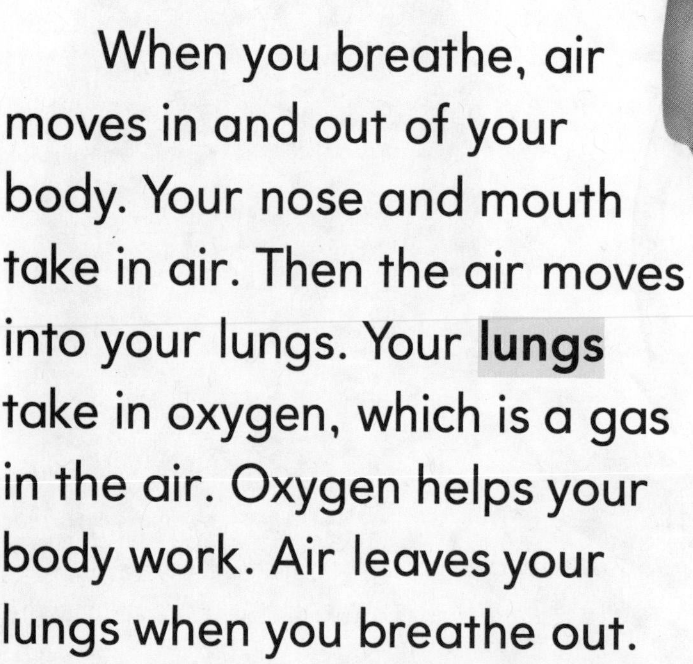

When you breathe, air moves in and out of your body. Your nose and mouth take in air. Then the air moves into your lungs. Your **lungs** take in oxygen, which is a gas in the air. Oxygen helps your body work. Air leaves your lungs when you breathe out.

▶ **Draw your lungs. Then draw arrows to show how air moves into your lungs.**

Your Heart

Your **heart** is a muscle.
pushes blood through
ur body. Blood carries
xygen and other things to
l parts of your body. Your
eart works all the time to
eep your blood flowing.

Your heart is in your chest, too.

▶ **Why is it important for your heart to beat all the time?**

Why It Matters

A Healthy Heart

Exercise is good for your body. Do you know why? One reason is that exercise keeps your heart strong.

Every time your heart beats, it pumps blood through your body. Exercise makes your heart beat faster and work harder. Over time, all this work makes your heart strong.

Take a Survey

Ask classmates which of these kinds of exercise they like the best. Use tallies to show their votes. Group your marks in fives.

Example 𝍸

Exercises We Like	Total
Running	III
Basketball	II
Swimming	𝍸 III
Soccer	III

Skip-count to find the total for each exercise. Then answer the questions.

1. Which exercise did most students like?

Swimming

2. How many votes did it get?

There is 7 for swimming. 7

Sum It Up »

1 Circle It!

Circle the words that tell about lungs.

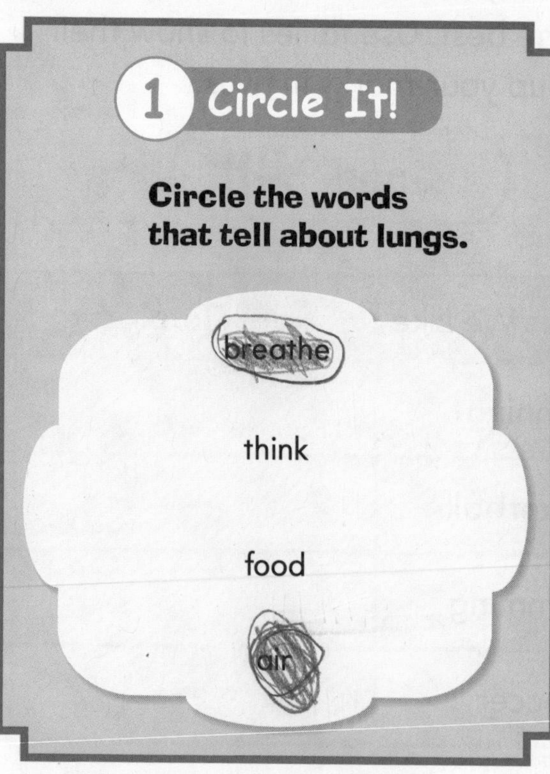

2 Write It!

Complete the poem.

I'm in charge of all your parts.

I'm the reason you are smart.

When you're at school, at play, or in bed,

I'm your brain______, and I'm in your head!

3 Draw It!

Draw yourself doing an exercise that helps keep your heart strong.

Brain Check

Name ____________________

Vocabulary Review

Label the body parts. Use each word in the word bank.

brain	heart	lungs	stomach	bone	muscle

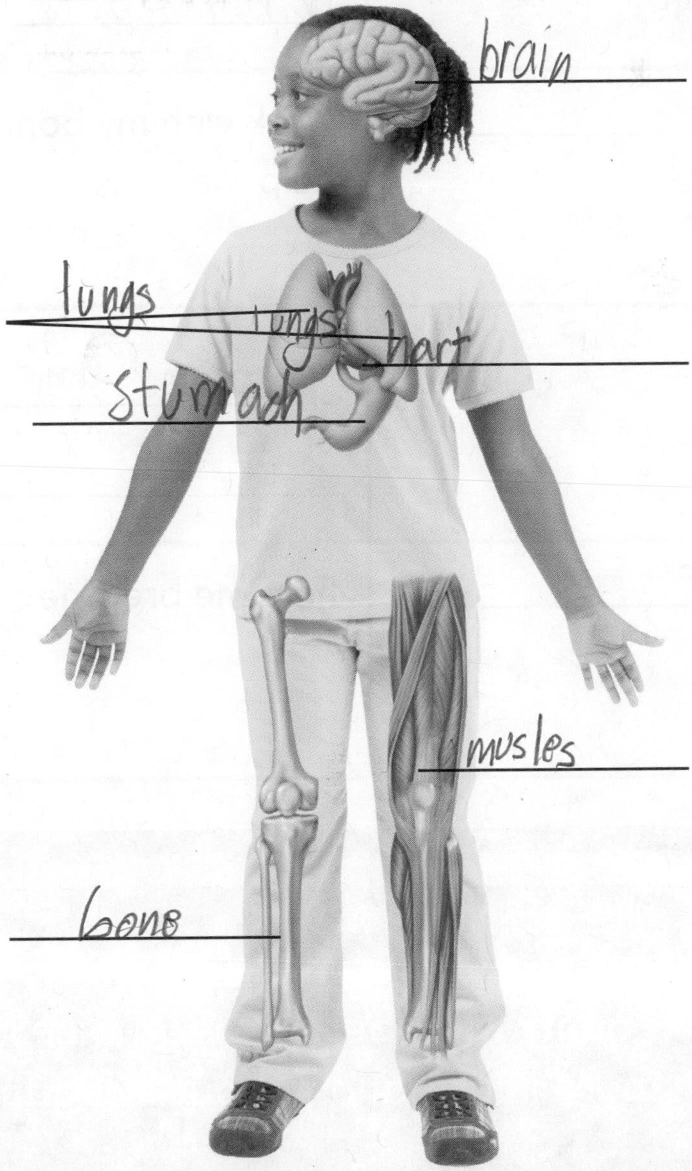

Apply Concepts

Fill in the chart. Show what you know about the parts of your body.

My Body

Part	What It Does
stomach	helps yov disalve your food
musles	work with my bones to help me move
skeleton	help me move
lungs	help me breathe

Family Members: *See ScienceSaurus®* for more information about living things.

SC.2.N.1.6 Explain how scientists alone or in groups are always investigating new ways to solve problems. SC.2.L.14.1 Distinguish human body parts (brain, heart, lungs, stomach, muscles, and skeleton) and their basic functions.
HE.2.C.1.5: Recognize the locations and functions of major human organs.

Get to Know . . . Dr. Patricia Bath

Dr. Patricia Bath is an eye doctor. She invented a machine that helps her operate on eyes. It uses a laser to remove cataracts. Cataracts can make a person's vision cloudy. They can even make people blind. Dr. Bath's machine has helped many people see again.

Fun Fact

The Snellen, the Landolt C, and the Lea test are three kinds of eye charts.

This Leads to That

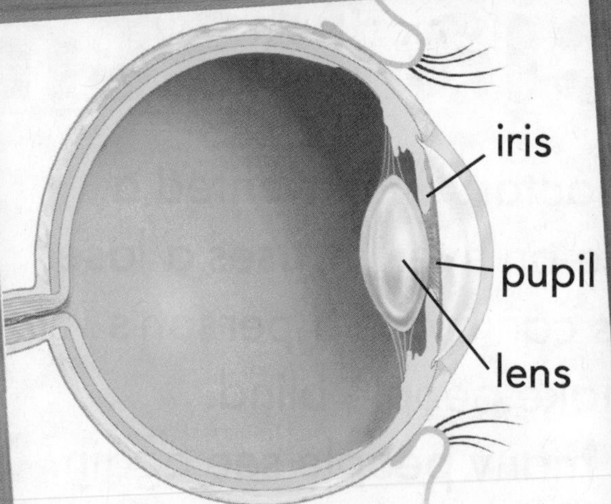

Cataracts affect the lens of the eye, which is behind the iris and the pupil. Dr. Bath's machine removes cataracts to help improve vision.

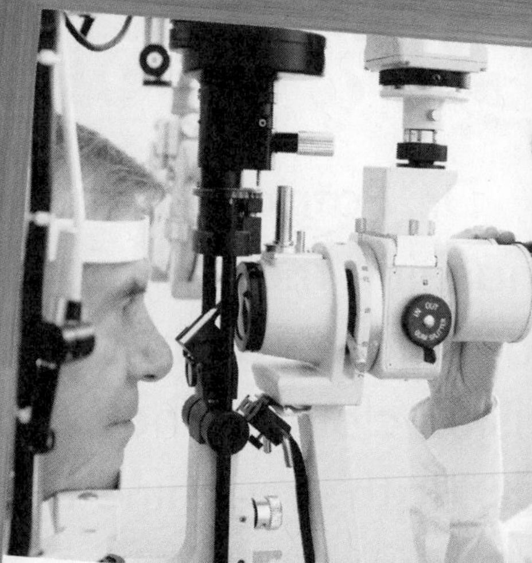

Dr. Bath still works to help people get better eye care. Here an eye doctor gives an older patient a checkup.

▶ What question would you ask Dr. Bath about her work?

___

___

___

SC.2.N.1.1 Raise questions ... investigate them in teams ... and generate appropriate explanations based on those explorations. SC.2.N.1.3 Ask "how do you know?" in appropriate situations ... SC.2.N.1.4 Explain how ... scientific investigations should yield similar conclusions ... SC.2.L.14.1 Distinguish human body parts (brain, heart, lungs, stomach, muscles, and skeleton) and their basic functions. HE.2.C.1.5 Recognize the locations and functions of major human organs.

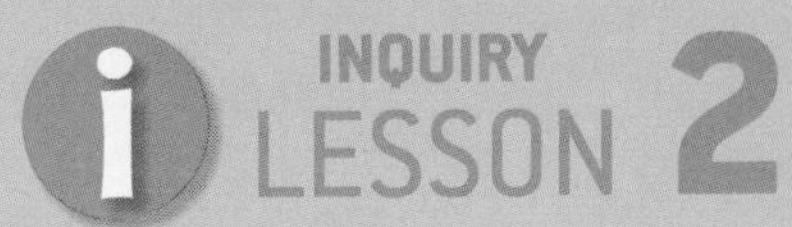

Name ______________________________

Essential Question

What Changes Your Heart Rate?

Materials

clock with second hand

EXPLORE

You can measure your heart rate. Then you can find how your heart rate changes.

Before You Begin—Preview the Steps

1. Find your heart rate. Work with a partner to count how many times your heart beats in 15 seconds. Record the number.
2. Do 20 jumping jacks.
3. Find your heart rate again. Count how many times it beats in 15 seconds. Record the number. Then compare the numbers.
4. Repeat the activity. Did you get the same results?

Set a Purpose

Write what you want to find out.

___

___

___

State Your Hypothesis

Write your hypothesis, or statement that you will test.

___

___

___

Think About the Procedure

How will you test the change in your heart rate?

___

___

___

Name ______________________

Record Your Data

Record your observations in this chart.

	Number of Heartbeats in 15 Seconds
Before Exercise	34 = 136 bpm
After Exercise	35 = 140 bpm

Show your data in a bar graph.

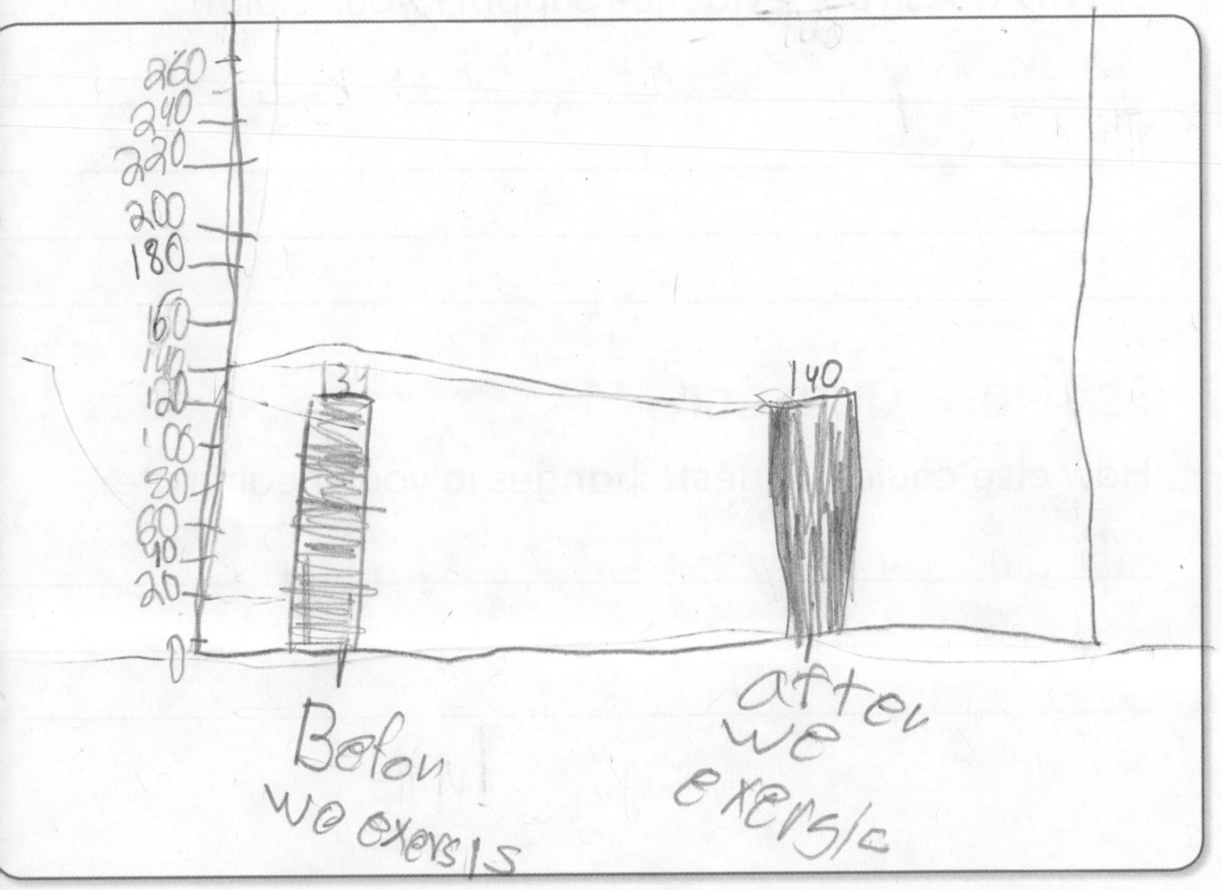

Claims • Evidence • Reasoning

1. Write a claim about how exercise affects your heart rate.

Exercising Makes your heart beat more faster.

2. What evidence supports your claim?

Befor exercising my heart beat 136 bmp. after exercising
after exercising it was 140 bmp.

3. Why does your evidence support your claim?

By trying it out you can find it out by doing exer-
Then your ansen.

Ask More Questions

How else could you test changes in your heart rate?

You can jump rope, pullups, blowing balowns, tatorshin
, and sports.

0

Life Cycles

alligator

I Wonder Why

Mother alligators bury their eggs in a nest. Why?
Turn the page to find out.

Here's Why

Mother alligators need to keep their eggs warm and protected for the young alligators to hatch.

Essential Questions and Florida Benchmarks

Science Notebook

Before you begin each lesson, write your thoughts about the Essential Question.

SC.2.L.16.1 Observe and describe major stages in the life cycles of plants and animals, including beans and butterflies.

LESSON 1

ssential Question

What Are Some Animal Life Cycles?

Engage Your Brain

Find the answer to the riddle in this lesson.

When is a frog not like a frog?

When it is a

_______________________.

Active Reading

Lesson Vocabulary

1 Preview the lesson.

2 Write the 6 vocabulary terms here.

_______________ _______________

_______________ _______________

_______________ _______________

Animal Start-Ups

A dog can have puppies. A cat can have kittens. Adult animals can **reproduce**, or have young. Animals such as puppies and kittens look like their parents. How does a kitten look like an adult cat?

Other young animals look very different from their parents. They go through changes and become like their parents.

A young butterfly does not look like its parents.

A young cat looks like its parents.

▶ **Name another animal that looks like its parents.**

Turtle

Vhat's in the Egg?

Many animals begin life by atching from an egg. Animals ıange as they grow. The ıanges that happen to an nimal during its life make up s **life cycle**.

▶ How are the animals in this chart alike?

____

____

Animal Life Cycles

Kind of Animal	Egg	Young	Adult
Chicken			
Turtle			
ainbow Trout			

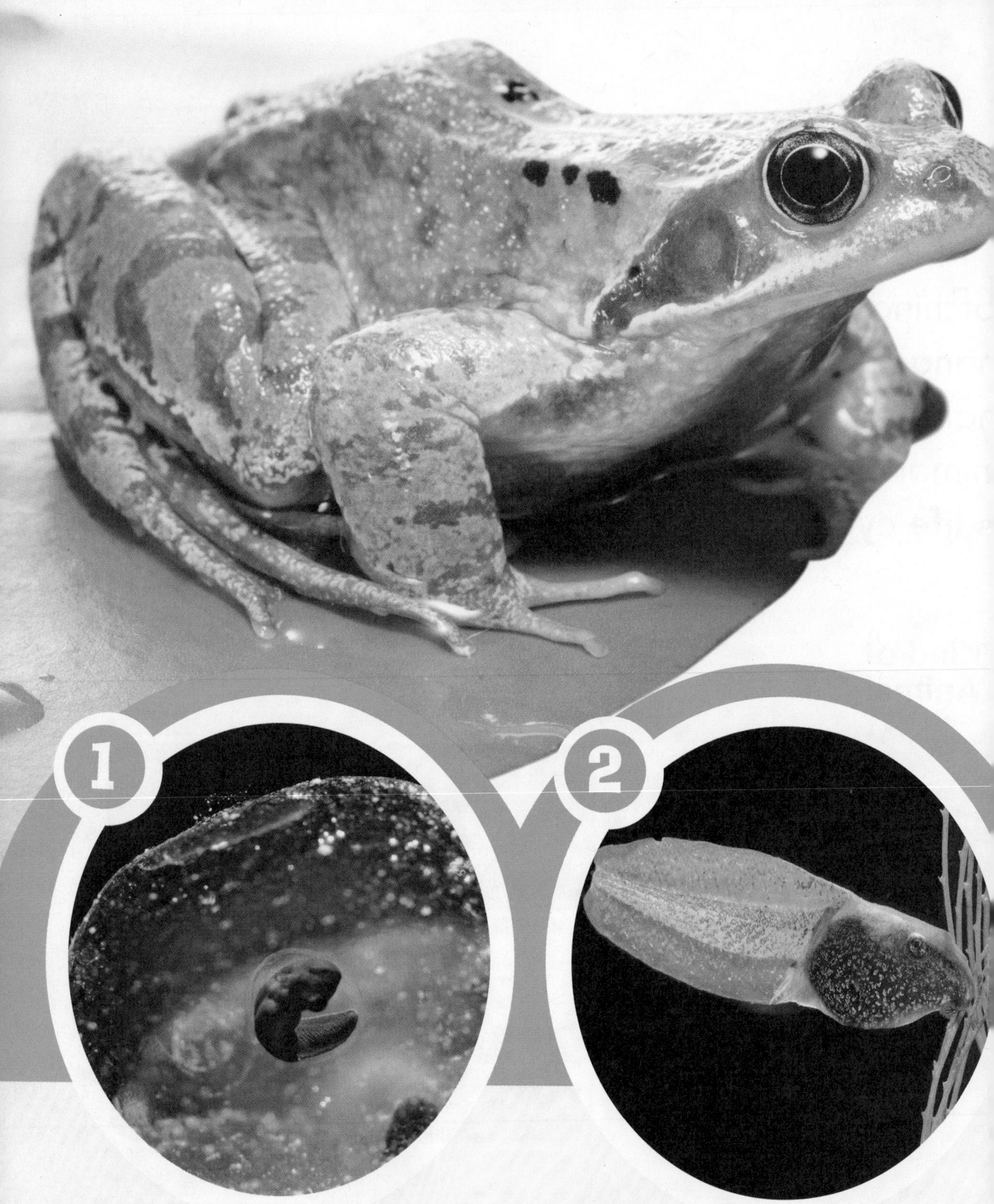

Egg

A frog begins life inside a tiny egg.

Young Tadpole

A **tadpole** hatches from the egg. It lives in water. It takes in oxygen with gills.

Hatch, Swim, Hop

Did you know that a frog begins life inside a tiny egg? The young frog goes through changes to become an adult. These changes are called **metamorphosis**.

Active Reading

Circle the name of the body parts that a tadpole uses to take in oxygen. Underline the name of the body parts that an adult frog uses to take in oxygen.

Growing Tadpole

The tadpole gets bigger. It grows four legs. Later, it loses its tail.

Frog

The adult can live on land or in the water. It hops. It breathes with lungs.

Polar Parenting

It is late October. A female polar bear gets a shelter ready for her cubs. She digs a den in the snow. The den will keep her young warm and safe. She gives birth in winter.

▶ **How is a polar bear's life cycle different from a frog's life cycle?**

look the same and they born alive.

Newborn

A polar bear cub is born inside the den. It drinks milk from its mother's body.

Growing Cub

The cub begins to explore outside the den.

Young Polar Bear

The young polar bear learns to swim and hunt.

Adult Polar Bear

The adult polar bear can live on its own. It can have its own young.

The Mighty Monarch

A monarch butterfly has a life cycle, too. An adult female butterfly lays a tiny egg. The egg is so small it is hard to see. This picture shows a close-up of an egg on a leaf.

▶ **Why do you think a butterfly egg is so small?**

A tiny **larva**, or caterpillar, hatches from the egg. A caterpillar is a young butterfly. The larva eats a lot and grows quickly.

Then the larva stops eating and moving. The larva becomes a pupa. It makes a hard covering.

A **pupa** goes through metamorphosis inside the covering. It grows wings. Many other changes also happen.

Finally, an adult butterfly comes out of the covering. It can have its own young.

Active Reading

Clue words can help you find the order of events. Draw a box around the clue words **then** and **finally**.

Sum It Up »

1 Mark It!

Draw an X on the animal that does not look like its young.

2 Draw It!

Draw a picture of this animal's mother.

3 Solve It!

Answer the riddle.

I am little now.
I will change and grow.
Someday I will be
an adult cat.

What am I?

____

4 Think About It!

Is a most like

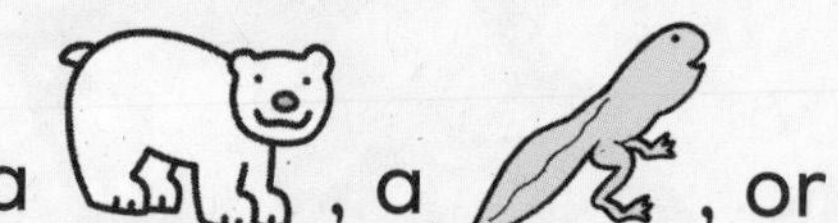

a , a , or

a ? Why?

Brain Check

LESSON **1**

Name ______________________________

Vocabulary Review

Use these words to complete the puzzle.

tadpole **change** **pupa** **larva** **reproduce** **cycle**

Across

1. The stage in a butterfly's life cycle after the egg
2. To make more living things of the same kind

Down

3. The stage in a butterfly's life between larva and adult
4. A young frog that lives in water
5. This takes place during metamorphosis in frogs and butterflies
6. All the stages of an animal's life make up its life __________.

Apply Concepts

How is the life cycle of a butterfly different from the life cycle of a polar bear? Use this chart to show your answer.

Life Cycles

Butterfly	Polar Bear
A butterfly hatches from an egg.	A polar bear is born alive
The ~~cater~~larva eats a leaf.	A polar bear cub drinks milk from its mother's body.
The larva goes throgh metamorphosis	A polar bear cub looks a lot like its parents.
A butterfly larva does not stay with its parents.	Bolorbear stay with parents for three years.

Family Members: *See ScienceSaurus®* for more information about living things.

Learn About ...

Salim Ali

Salim Ali is called the "Birdman of India." He traveled around India to study birds in their habitats. Ali discovered some kinds of birds. He wrote books about the birds he observed. Many people enjoyed reading his books.

...Fun Fact

Bird watchers use binoculars like these to see birds more closely.

Watch the Bird Grow!

Salim Ali learned about birds. You can learn about birds, too.

▶ **Order the life cycle of a robin. Number the pictures from 1 to 4.**

___

young robin

___

adult robin

___

robin chick

___

robin eggs

▶ **How is a robin's life cycle like the life cycles of other animals you know?**

____

____

____

____

____

____

SC.2.N.1.1 Raise questions ... investigate them in teams ... and generate appropriate explanations based on those explorations. SC.2.N.1.3 Ask "how do you know?" in appropriate situations ... SC.2.L.16.1 Observe and describe major stages in the life cycles of plants and animals, including beans and butterflies.

INQUIRY LESSON 2

Name ______________________________

'ssential Question

How Does a Bean Plant Grow?

Materials

pencil
soil in cup
beans
water

XPLORE

ou can grow your own bean plant! Observe how the plant changes as grows.

Before You Begin—Preview the Steps

1. Use the pencil to make holes in the soil. Place a bean in each hole. Cover the beans with soil.
2. Water the soil. Place the cup in a warm, sunny place.
3. Observe the cup each day for two weeks. Water the soil when it is dry.

Set a Purpose

Explain what you will learn from this activity.

Think About the Procedure

1. Why must you give the plant water and sunlight?

2. Compare the way that your bean plant grew with the way that a classmate's bean plant grew. What was the same?

Name ___________________________

Record Your Data

Write and draw to record your observations in this chart.

Date	Observations

Claims • Evidence • Reasoning

1. Write a claim about how a bean plant changes during its life cycle.

2. What evidence supports your claim?

3. Why does your evidence support your claim?

Ask More Questions

What other questions can you ask about how plants grow?

SC.2.L.16.1 Observe and describe major stages in the life cycles of plants and animals, including beans and butterflies.

LESSON 3

Essential Question

What Are Some Plant Life Cycles?

Engage Your Brain

Find the answer to the question in this lesson.

What does the flower part of a dandelion make?

It makes

______________________.

Active Reading

Lesson Vocabulary

1 Preview the lesson.

2 Write the 4 vocabulary terms here.

______________ ______________

______________ ______________

Plant Start-Ups

Plants are living things. They grow and change. They have life cycles. Most plant life cycles begin with a **seed**. New plants grow from seeds. The growing plants start to look like their parent plants.

Active Reading

Find the words that tell about seeds. Draw a line under the words.

The plants in this garden grew from seeds.

How Fast Do Plants Grow?

Some plants grow quickly. Plants in a vegetable garden take just a few months to become adult plants. Other plants, such as trees, take many years to become adults.

Do the Math

Interpret a Table

Use the chart to answer the question.

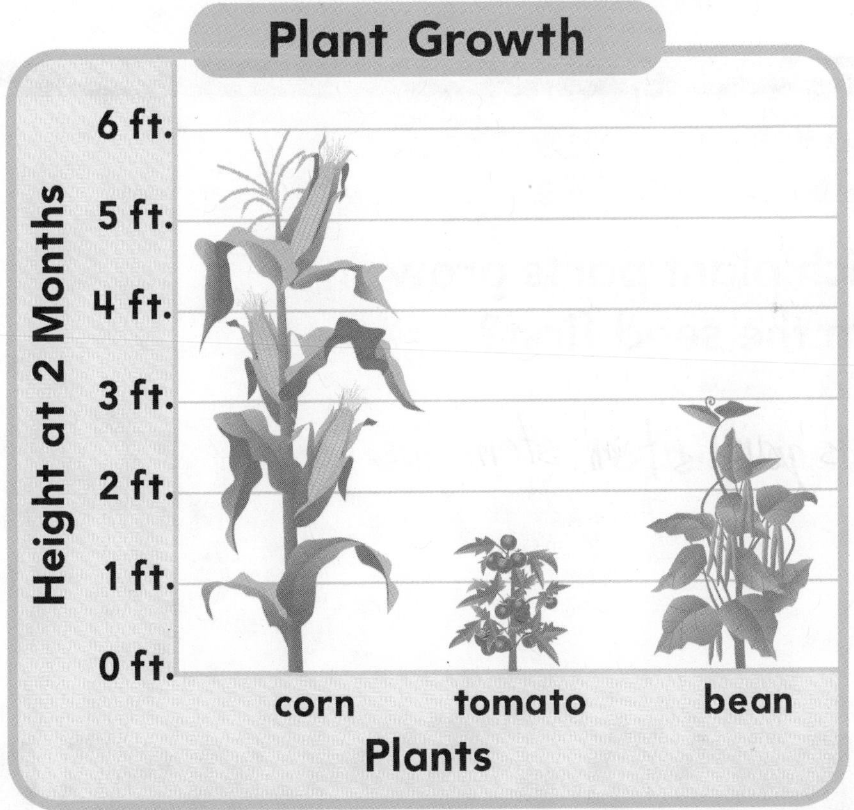

▶ How much taller did the corn plant grow than the bean plant?

Start with a Seed

What happens when you plant a seed? When a seed gets warmth, air, and water, it may germinate. **Germinate** means to start to grow. The stem of the tiny plant breaks through the ground. The plant gets taller and grows leaves.

▶ **Which plant parts grow from the seed first?**

the roots and stem stem gose up.

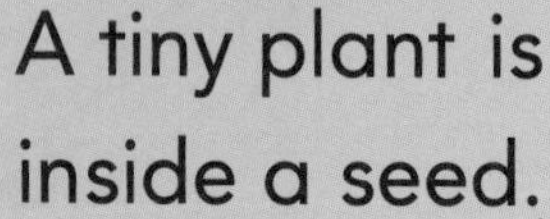

A tiny plant is inside a seed.

The seed germinates. The roots grow down.

The stem grows up toward the light.

Growing Up

The tiny plant inside the seed has become a young plant called a **seedling**.

The seedling grows into an adult plant. An adult plant can make flowers and seeds.

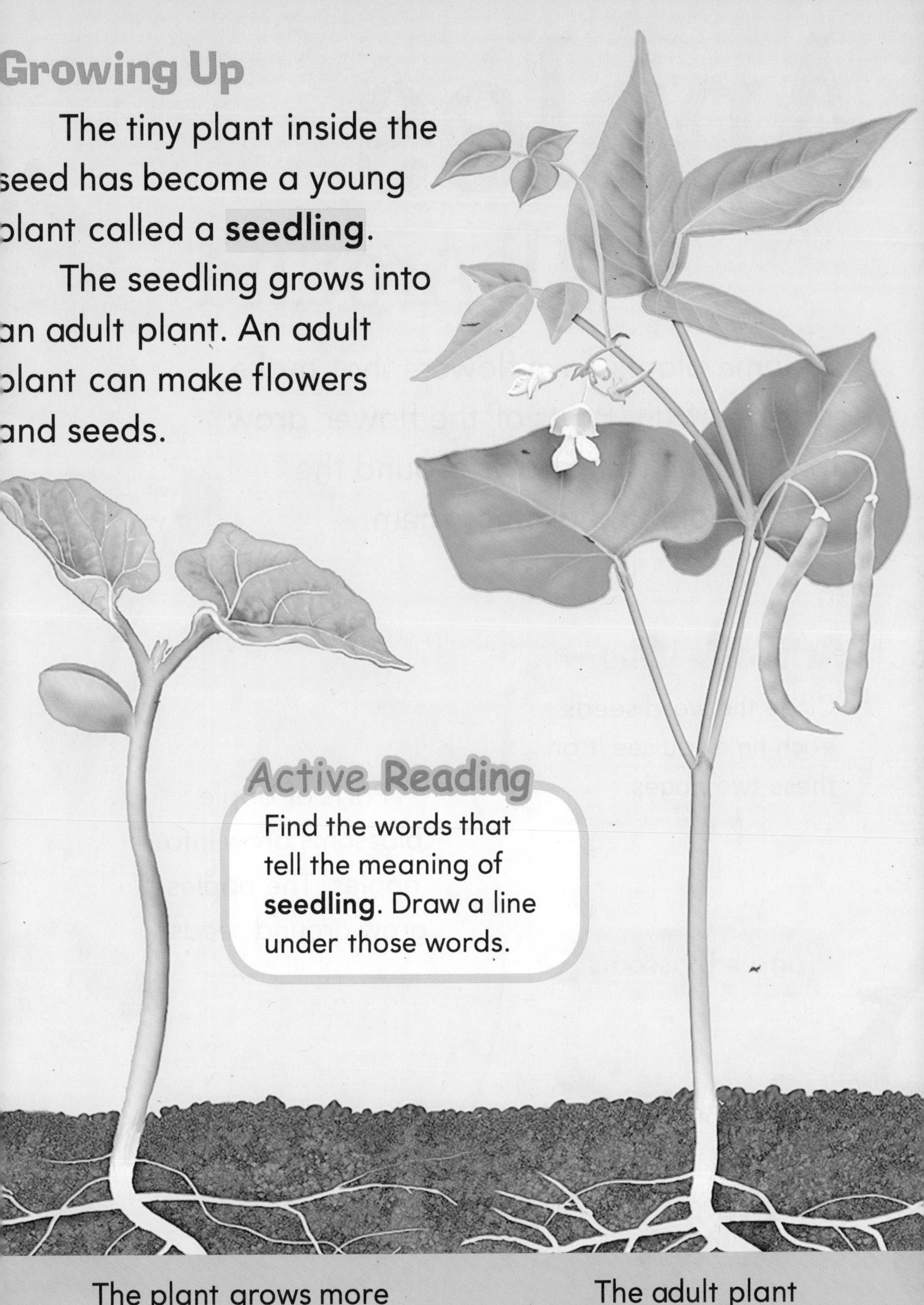

Active Reading

Find the words that tell the meaning of **seedling**. Draw a line under those words.

The plant grows more roots and leaves.

The adult plant grows flowers.

Apples All Around

Some plants have flowers that make seeds and fruit. Parts of the flower grow into fruit. The fruit grows around the seeds to hold and protect them.

Active Reading

Circle the word **seeds** each time you see it on these two pages.

apple blossoms

Parts of apple blossoms grow into apples. The apples grow around seeds.

A Long Life

Some plants have short lives. They die soon after their flowers make seeds. Other plants, such as apple trees, can live for many years. An apple tree can live for a hundred years or more!

adult apple tree

▶ What do apple blossoms make?

____

Inside a Cone

Some plants, like pine trees, do not have flowers. But they do have seeds. Where do their seeds grow? A **cone** is a part of a pine tree and some other plants. Seeds grow inside the cone.

closed pinecones

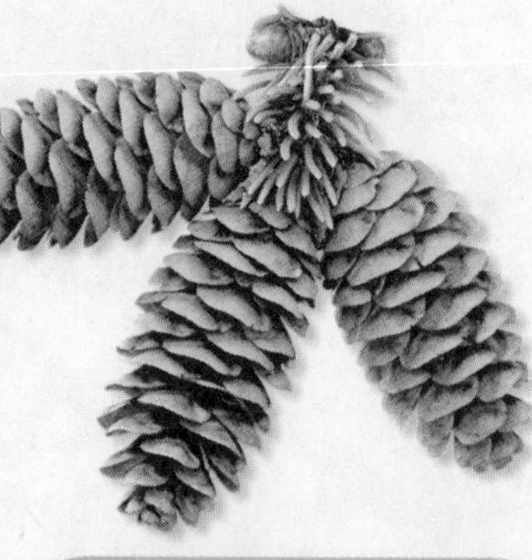

open pinecones with seeds

The cone protects the seeds until they are ready to germinate. Then the cone opens up, and the seeds can fall out.

▶ **Where do pine seeds form?**

Pine Tree Beginnings

Pine seeds fall to the ground and germinate. As the seedlings grow, they start to look like their parent plants. After a few years, the pine trees grow cones and make seeds. The life cycle begins again.

▶ **What happens after an adult pine tree grows cones and makes seeds?**

____

____

Sum It Up »

1 Draw It!

Draw the missing step in the plant's life cycle. Label your picture.

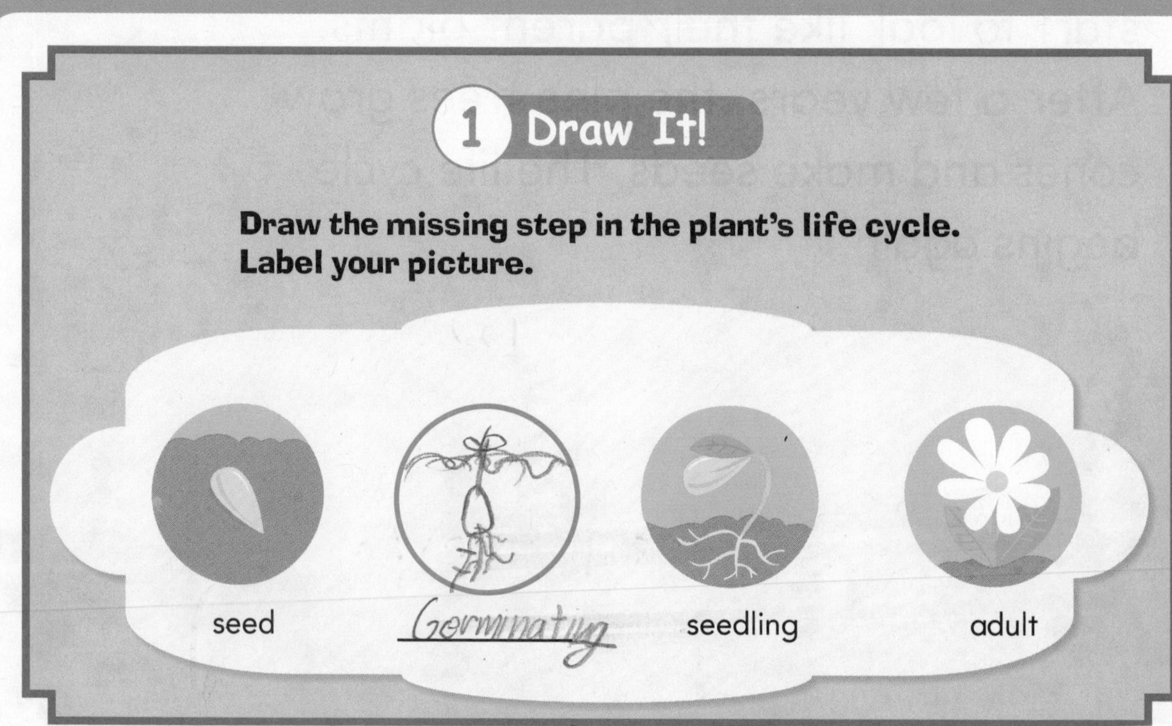

2 Mark It!

Draw an X on the plant part that does not have seeds.

3 Think About It!

How are flowers and pinecones alike?

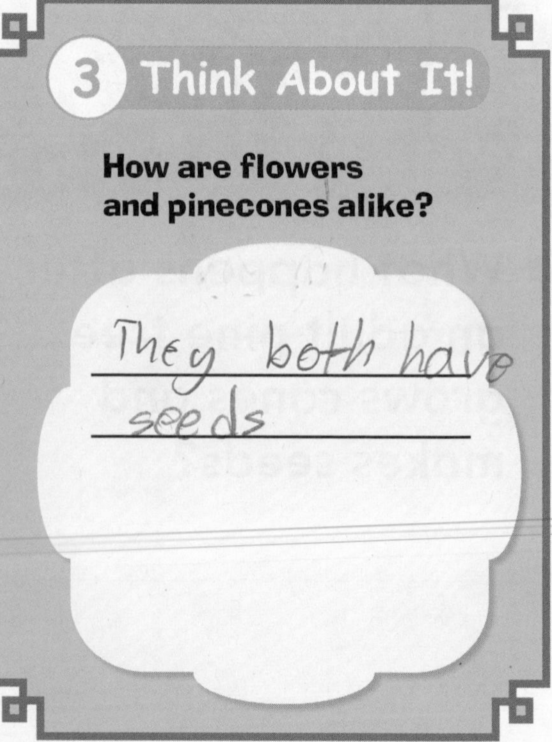

Brain Check

LESSON 3

Name ______________________________

Vocabulary Review

Read each word. Trace a path through the maze to connect each word to its picture.

seed cone flower seedling

Apply Concepts

Write to tell about the life cycle of a plant. Use the words germinate, seed, and seedling.

Family Members: Ask your child to tell you about plant life cycles. Then take a walk around your neighborhood. Talk about the plants you see.

SC.2.N.1.1 Raise questions ... investigate them in teams ... and generate appropriate explanations based on those explorations. **SC.2.N.1.3** Ask "how do you know?" in appropriate situations. **SC.2.L.16.1** Observe and describe major stages in the life cycles of plants and animals, including beans and butterflies.

S.T.E.M.

ENGINEERING & TECHNOLOGY

On the Farm

Farm System

A farm is a kind of system. A system is a group of parts that work together. All parts must work for the whole system to run well. Some parts of a farm are the crops, animals, people, and tools.

Farmers use tools, such as fences, to care for their crops and animals.

Farmers plan where to plant crops. They know what times of year are best to plant.

S.T.E.M. (continued)

What to Do?

Read the story. Then write how you would solve the problem.

You have a small farm. Everything is working well. One day, wind knocks down part of a fence on your farm.

1. How could the broken fence affect the farm?
2. What would you do to fix the problem?
3. How do you think your solution will help?

1. ______________________________

____

____

2. ______________________________

____

____

3. ______________________________

____

____

Design It: Guard the Lettuce!

Follow the steps of the design process to solve the problem.

What's the Problem?

Rabbits keep eating the lettuce in your garden. What can you do to protect the lettuce?

What's the Solution?

Try building a lettuce protector. Think about what you need to build the protector.

▼ Rabbits eat lettuce and other leafy plants.

Make It:

These materials might help you get started.

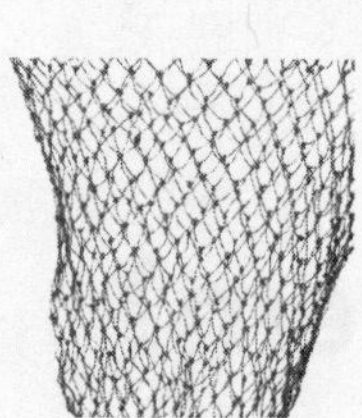

1. Make a test garden with two plants.
2. Build a protector for the plants. Draw your design.
3. Test your protector. How could you improve it?
4. Draw and write about your design and results in your Science Notebook.

11 Basic Needs and Environments

parrotfish near the Florida Keys

FLORIDA BIG IDEA 17

Interdependence

I Wonder Why

This parrotfish is eating underwater. Why?
Turn the page to find out.

Here's Why

Parrotfish live in water environments. They eat algae on underwater coral reefs.

Essential Questions and Florida Benchmarks

Science Notebook

Before you begin each lesson, write your thoughts about the Essential Question.

SC.2.L.17.1 Compare and contrast the basic needs that all living things, including humans, have for survival.

LESSON 1

Essential Question

What Are Plant Needs?

Engage Your Brain

Find the answer to the question in the lesson.

What do you know about a pumpkin this big?

Its

____

were met.

Active Reading

Lesson Vocabulary

1 Preview the lesson.

2 Write the 2 vocabulary terms here.

________________ ________________

Plant Needs

Plants are living things. All living things must have certain things to live and grow. These things are called **basic needs**. What happens if a plant does not meet its basic needs? It may stop growing. It may turn brown or begin to droop. It may die.

Active Reading

Circle details that tell what happens when a plant does not meet its basic needs.

These plants are meeting their basic needs.

▶ What basic need is the boy giving the plants?

People can help plants meet their basic needs.

Wonderful Water

Plants need water. Do you know how they get it? A plant's roots take in water from the soil. Water is a basic need that helps plants live and grow.

Light and Airy

Do you wonder why people put some potted plants by windows? Plants need sunlight to grow. They also need air and water. Plants use air, water, and sunlight to make their own food.

Active Reading

Underline the sentence that tells what plants need to make food.

How are these plants getting what they need?

Nutrients and Space

Plants need nutrients from the soil. **Nutrients** are substances that help plants grow. Growing plants need more nutrients and water. Their roots grow and spread to get more of these things. Plants need enough space for their roots, stems, and leaves to grow.

Sum It Up »

3 Draw It!

Draw a picture of a plant. Label the picture to show that the plant is getting what it needs.

Name ____________________

Vocabulary Review

Find and circle the words in this word search. Then answer the question.

sunlight ✓ **water** ✓ **soil** ✓ **air** ✓ **space** ✓ **nutrients** ✓

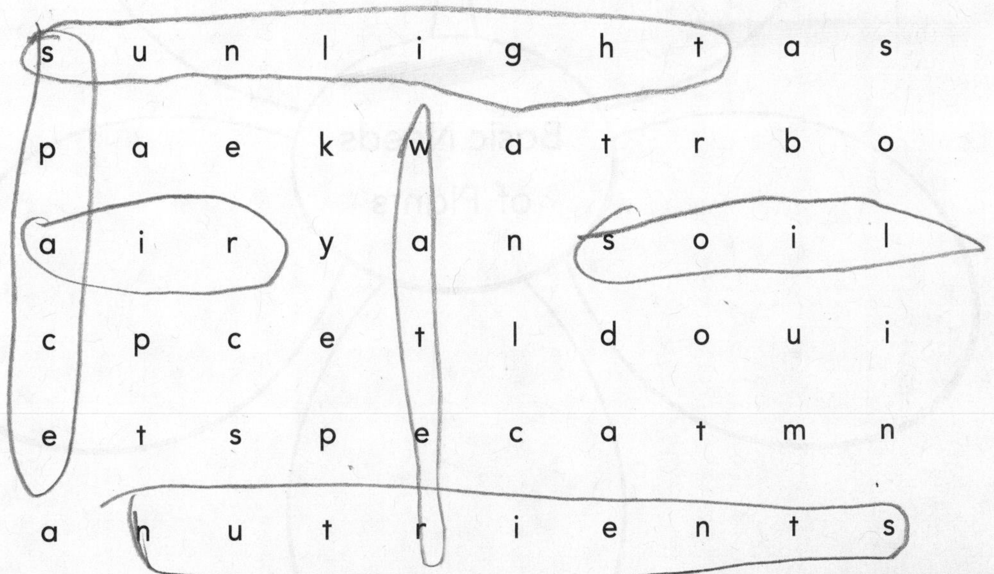

s	u	n	l	i	g	h	t	a	s
p	a	e	k	w	a	t	r	b	o
a	i	r	y	a	n	s	o	i	l
c	p	c	e	t	l	d	o	u	i
e	t	s	p	e	c	a	t	m	n
a	n	u	t	r	i	e	n	t	s

What are the things that plants must meet to live and grow?

Water and sun and space

Apply Concepts

Complete the word web to tell about the things that plants need.

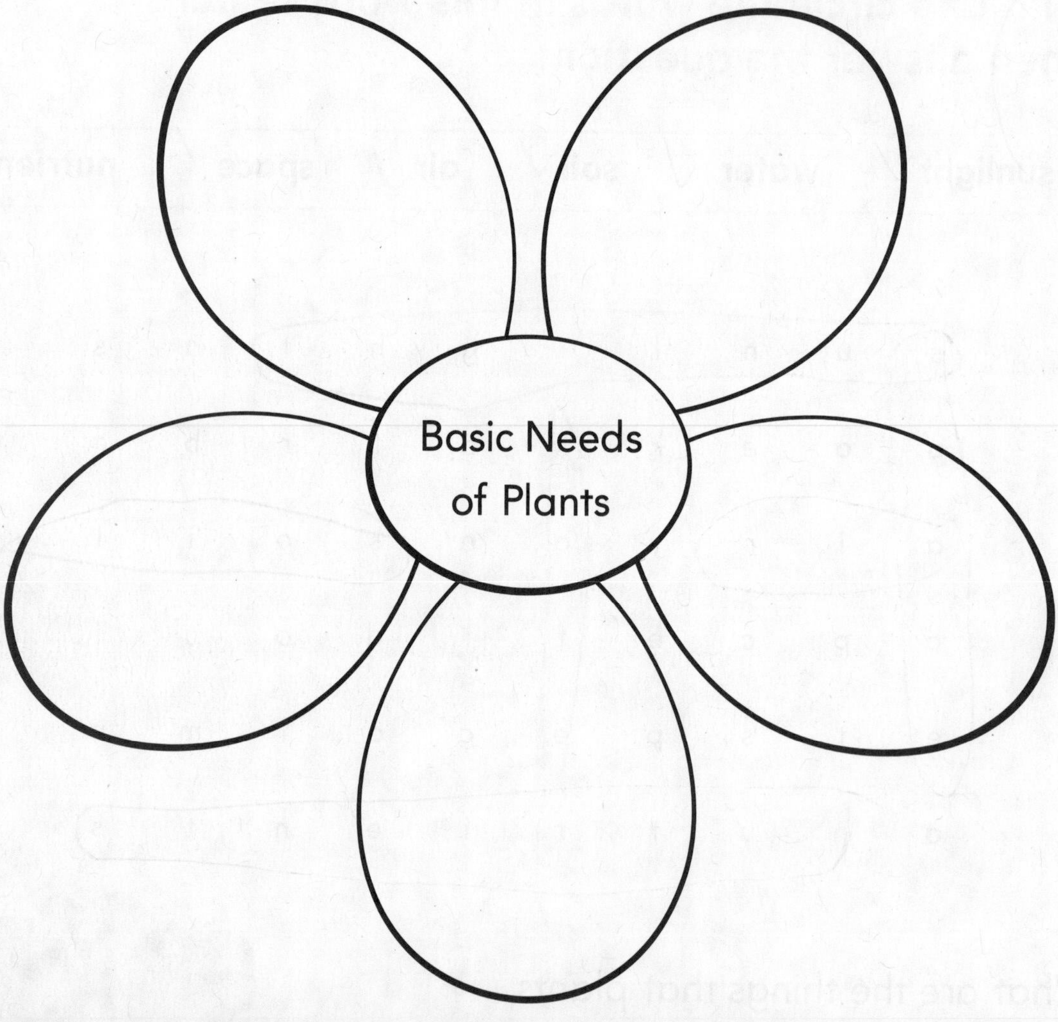

Basic Needs of Plants

Family Members: See *ScienceSaurus*® for more information about plants.

Essential Question

What Are Animal Needs?

Engage Your Brain

Find the answer to the question in the lesson.

How is a frog like a human?

Both need food to ______________.

Active Reading

Lesson Vocabulary

1. Preview the lesson.
2. Write the 4 vocabulary terms here.

______________ ______________

______________ ______________

Just the Basics

Animals are living things. Humans are living things, too. Just like plants, animals and humans have basic needs. They must meet their basic needs in order to **survive**, or stay alive.

What basic need are these animals getting? How does this make animals like plants?

Active Reading

Circle the words that help you know what **survive** means.

Animals need water to survive.

Water Everywhere

Humans need water, too. Drinking water helps us survive. Water is also in other things we drink, such as milk and juice.

The water in this drink helps the girl get what she needs.

Draw and label a picture to show what you like to drink.

It's in the Air!

Living things need oxygen to survive. Humans and many animals use body parts called **lungs** to get oxygen from the air. Humans and these animals take in the air through their mouths and noses.

Put a hand on your chest and take a deep breath. Can you feel your lungs taking in air?

This boy is swimming underwater. He is using a snorkel.

▶ Why do people need a snorkel to swim underwater?

____

____

t's in the Water!

Some animals, such as fish, use
s to take in oxygen. **Gills** are
rts of an animal that take in
ygen from the water. Can you
d the gill on the side of the
h's head?

▶ Label the part of the fish that takes in oxygen.

Do the Math

Interpret a Table

Animal Breathing Rates

Use the chart to answer the questions.

Animal Name	Breaths per Minute
cat	25
dog	20
sparrow	50
horse	15

1. How many more breaths per minute does a sparrow take than a cat?

2. How many more breaths per minute does a dog take than a horse?

Food for Thought

Food is an important need for animals and humans. Food helps animals and humans grow and change. Some animals eat plants. Some eat other animals. Other animals and humans may eat both plants and animals.

A giraffe eats the leaves from trees.

▶ Draw a food you like to eat.

Protection for All

Animals need space to move, find food, and grow. Humans and many animals also need shelter. A **shelter** is a safe place to live.

Humans also need something that animals do not need. We need clothes to protect our bodies from cold and rainy weather.

Kinds of Shelters

Some bears live in dens.

Some bees live in hives.

A prairie dog lives in a burrow.

Some humans live in houses.

Active Reading

Circle the words that name different shelters.

Sum It Up »

1 Circle It!

Circle the living thing that does not use lungs to get oxygen.

2 Mark It!

Cross out the thing that humans do not need to survive.

3 Draw It!

Draw an animal in its shelter. Show the animal meeting another need.

LESSON 2

Name ____________________

Vocabulary Review

Read the words and the clues.
Write the word that goes with each clue.

lungs	gills	shelter	survive	oxygen

1. I am a safe place to live. s h e l t e r
2. We are the body parts that you use to take in oxygen. l u n g s
3. I mean to stay alive. s u r v i v e
4. We are the body parts that fish and tadpoles use to stay alive in water. g i l l s
5. I am in the air you breathe. o x y g e n

Apply Concepts

Complete the Venn diagram. Show how animal needs and plant needs are alike and different.

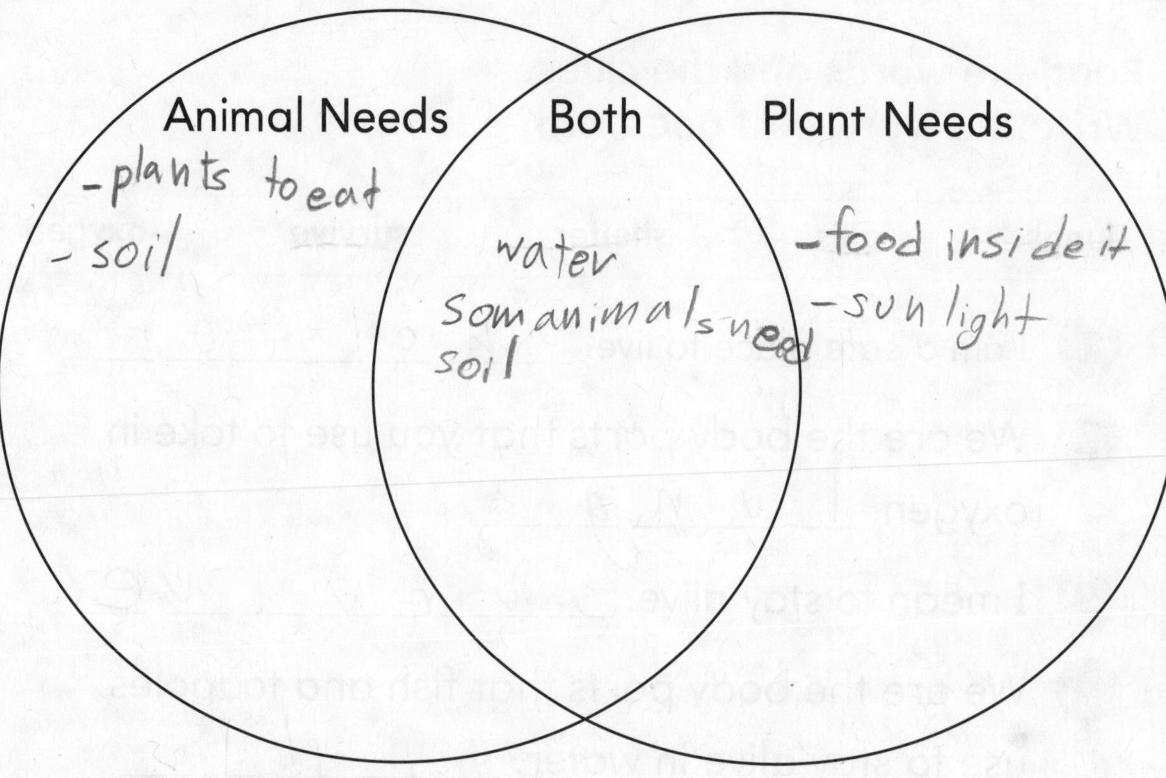

Complete the sentence.
Tell about the main idea of this lesson.

Basic needs are the things that animals and plants need to _____________.

Family Members: See *ScienceSaurus*® for more information about animals.

SC.2.N.1.1 Raise questions ... investigate them in teams ... and generate appropriate explanations based on those explorations. SC.2.N.1.2 Compare the observations made ... using the same tools. SC.2.N.1.3 Ask "how do you know?" in appropriate situations.

S.T.E.M.

ENGINEERING & TECHNOLOGY

Tool Time

How We Use Tools

Tools are objects that people use to make a job easier. People can use tools to meet needs.

One need is shelter. A shelter may be a house. People use many tools to build a house.

The Best Tool for the Job

Draw a line to match each tool to how it is used.

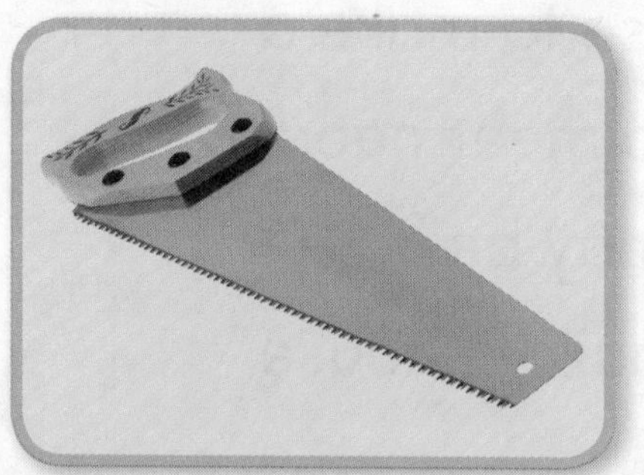

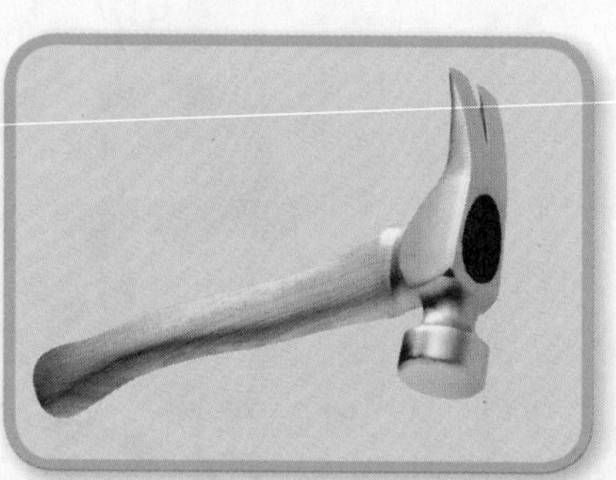

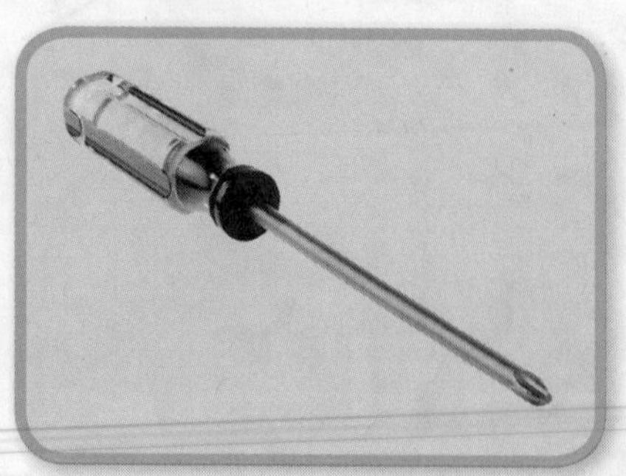

ENGINEERING DESIGN CHALLENGE

Design It: A New Tool

People use tools at home. They may use tools to clean up. What kind of tool could pick up toys from the floor? Design one to find out!

▶ A broom is a tool that helps clean the floor.

S.T.E.M. (continued)

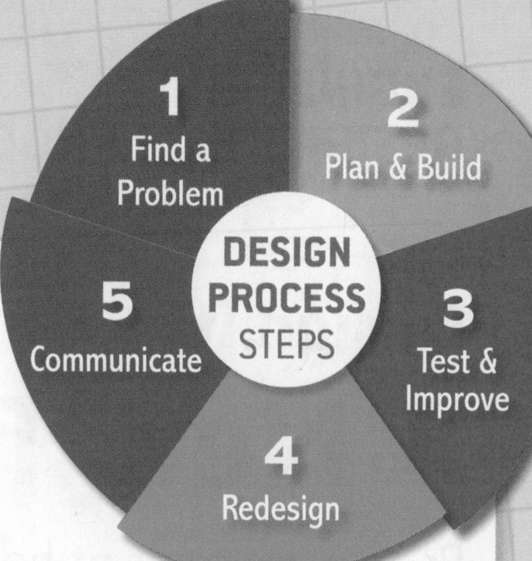

What to Do:

1. Think about what parts the tool will need.
2. Draw a picture of your design.
3. Label the parts.
4. How does the tool work?
5. Write about your tool in your Science Notebook.

SC.2.N.1.1 Raise questions . . . investigate them in teams . . . and generate appropriate explanations based on those explorations. SC.2.N.1.3 Ask "how do you know?" in appropriate situations . . . . SC.2.N.1.4 Explain how . . . scientific investigations should yield similar conclusions . . . . SC.2.N.1.5 Distinguish between empirical observation . . . and ideas or inferences . . . . SC.2.L.17.2 Recognize . . . living things are found all over Earth . . . live in habitats that meet its basic needs.

Name ______________________________

ssential Question

an Plants urvive in ifferent nvironments?

Materials

2 desert plants

measuring cup

XPLORE

Vhat happens to a desert plant in a ain forest environment? Let's find out.

efore You Begin—Preview the Steps

1 Label one plant **desert**. Label the other plant **rain forest**. Place both plants in a sunny window.

2 Water the desert plant once. Give it $\frac{1}{4}$ cup of water. Water the rain forest plant each day. Give it $\frac{1}{4}$ cup of water in the morning, at noon, and in the afternoon.

3 Predict what you think will happen to each plant. Observe the plants for one week. Record any changes you observe.

Set a Purpose

Write what you want to find out.

____

____

Make a Prediction

Write a prediction about what you think will happen.

____

____

Think About the Procedure

1. Why will you water the desert plant only once?

____

Think About the Procedure

2. Why will you water the rain forest plant three times a day?

____

____

Name ____________________

ecord Your Data

Vrite and draw to record your observations in this chart.

Date	Observations

Claims • Evidence • Reasoning

1. Write a claim about whether a plant from one environment can live in a different environment?

2. What evidence supports your claim?

3. Why does your evidence support your claim?

Ask More Questions

What other questions can you ask about plants in different environments?

SC.2.N.1.6 Explain how scientists alone or in groups are always investigating new ways to solve problems. SC.2.L.17.1 Compare and contrast the basic needs that all living things, including humans, have for survival.

Ask an Environmental Scientist

What do environmental scientists do?
We study the harmful effects to different kinds of environments.

How do environmental scientists help wildlife?
We find problems that affect wildlife and people in the environments. We figure out ways to solve them.

Sometimes people can harm an environment. For example, a factory may put waste into a stream. This may kill fish. We help the factory find other ways to get rid of its waste.

Now It's Your Turn!

▶ What question would you ask an environmental scientist?

____

____

____

Making Environments Better

▶ **Draw or write the answer to each question.**

1 What do you think is most interesting about what environmental scientists do?

2 What might be difficult about what they do?

3 Why are environmental scientists important?

4 Think about being an environmental scientist. Draw an environment you would like to study.

1

2

3

4

SC.2.L.17.2 Recognize and explain that living things are found all over Earth, but each is only able to live in habitats that meet its basic needs.

ssential Question

Where Do Plants and Animals Live?

Engage Your Brain

Find the answer to the question in the lesson.

What kind of environment does this fish live in?

It lives in the

________________.

Active Reading

Lesson Vocabulary

1 Preview the lesson.

2 Write the 2 vocabulary terms here.

________________ ________________

All Around You

Look around you. All the living and nonliving things you see make up your **environment**. Living things from one environment usually cannot live in a different one. They live in the environment that meets their needs.

A **habitat** is a smaller part of an environment. A habitat is the place where a living thing gets the food, water, and shelter it needs.

Active Reading

Circle the words that tell what a **habitat** is.

Some fox kits live in a forest environment.

Salty Water

An ocean environment is a large body of salt water. The top layer of the ocean has the most living things. Here, plants get the sunlight they need, and animals find food. There is no sunlight in the deepest parts of the ocean.

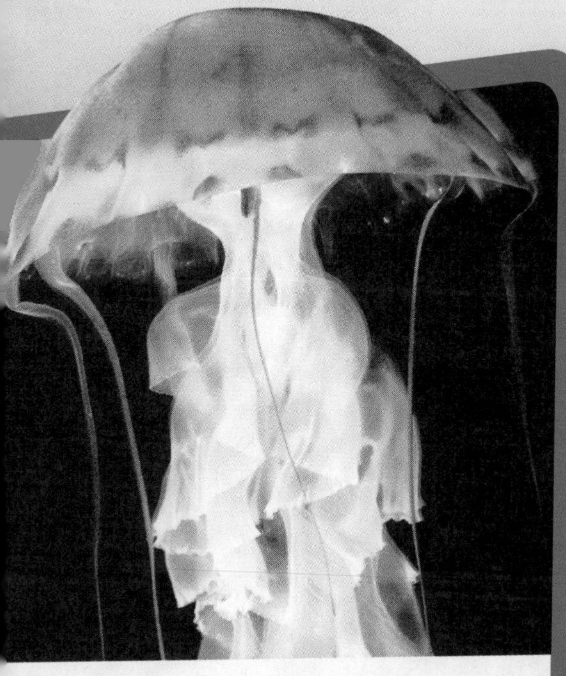

A jellyfish's tentacles sting and catch its food.

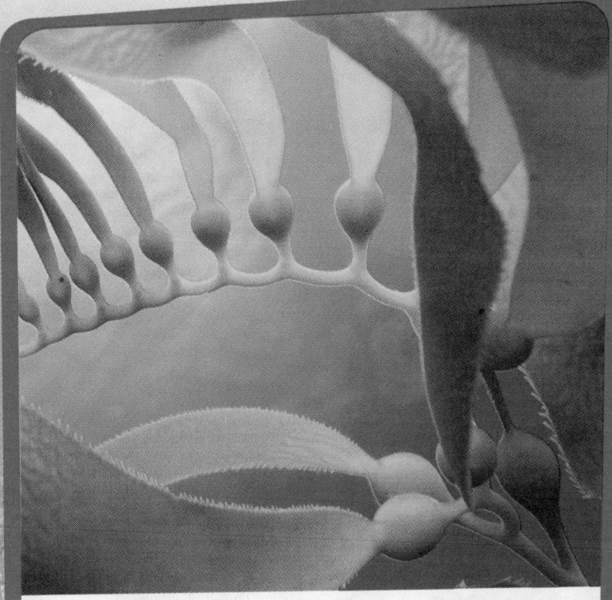

Kelp makes its own food. Many animals eat it.

▶ **Why do plants live near the top layer of the ocean?**

____

____

In a Rain Forest

A rain forest gets a lot of rain. The trees grow tall and block the sun. The plants on the forest floor do not need much sunlight. Animals, such as monkeys and birds, can use the tall trees as habitats.

These living things can live in the rain forest because it meets their needs.

▶ **Draw a rain forest animal that might live in the trees.**

Dry As a Bone

A desert environment s very dry and gets little ain. Desert plants store vater in their thick stems or leaves. In hot deserts, many animals hide during the day.

A Joshua tree can be a habitat for birds, insects, and small animals.

Desert plants and animals can survive with little water.

desert hare

Gila monster

▶Draw a cactus.

cactus

It's Cold Out Here!

A tundra environment is a very cold and snowy place. Plants and shrubs grow close together and low to the ground. Animals have thick fur that helps keep them warm.

An Arctic fox's white fur is hard to see against the snow.

purple saxifrage flowers

▶ **How does an Arctic fox's white fur help it in winter?**

by ceeping it warm

On the Prairie

Tall grasses and wildflowers live in a prairie environment. A prairie is mostly dry with just a few kinds of trees or shrubs. Large animals eat the grasses. Smaller animals and insects find habitats among the grasses.

Active Reading

Read the labels. Circle the name of the animal that finds food and shelter in prairie grasses.

Bison travel in herds and eat prairie grasses.

coneflowers

prairie dogs

red-tailed hawk

Sum It Up »

1 Draw It!

Choose an environment. Draw the living and nonliving things in that environment.

2 Label It!

Name the environment in which you would find each living thing.

water

besert

rainforest

Brain Check

Name ____________________

Vocabulary Review

Use the words below to complete the puzzle.

habitat desert environment rain forest tundra prairie

Across

1 a cold, snowy environment

2 a dry, grassy environment

3 a dry environment

Down

4 all the living and nonliving things in a place

5 an environment with tall trees and lots of rain

6 a place where a living thing has the food, water, and shelter it needs to live

Apply Concepts

Write two details that go with the main idea. One detail should be about animals in that environment. The other should be about plants in that environment. Then answer the question.

Main Idea
A tundra is a cold, snowy environment.

Detail	Detail
The artic Fox is wite.	there is notany plauts

What do all the living and nonliving things in a place make up? evermont

Family Members: Talk about your environment with your child. What living and nonliving things do you see? Look for small habitats in your area.

21st Century Skills

Technology and Coding

Have you ever wondered how video games are made? Or how a cell phone works? If so, you might like computer science! Computer science is the study of computer technology.

What Computers Can Do

Computers are machines that take in, manage, and store information. You can solve math problems with a computer. You can make art or music with a computer. Computers can do many things.

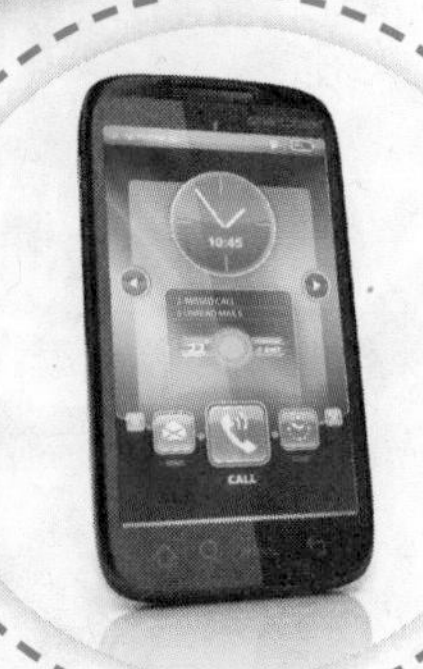

Do you recognize these objects? They use computer technology.

Computers are all around you. Even some toasters and cars use computer technology!

Draw another
example here.

Let's Talk!

How do computers help solve problems? They follow instructions, or programs, that people make.

Programs are written in a special language, or code. Computers understand the code and follow its instructions. If you learn the code, you can write computer programs, too!

```
dog.speed = 5;
play_sound(woof);
```

People who work in computer science have many skills. They are creative and like to solve problems.

Designing and writing a computer program is like solving a puzzle. The computer follows the program's instructions exactly and in order. If something is missing, the program won't work as planned.

How would you move the player to the treasure chest? Explain the steps.

____

____

____

Play it Safe

Be careful with electronics. Protect them from dust, dirt, and water. Dropping a device can damage it.

Electricity can be dangerous. If you see damaged cables, do not touch them. Tell an adult.

Limit the time you spend on electronics. Take breaks to exercise or stretch.

Talk to your family about rules for the Internet. Do not share private information on your computer or phone. This includes pictures and passwords.

Circle the pictures that show how to use electronics safely. Place an X over the pictures that do not.

Careers in Computing

Do you like art and working with computers? If so, you might enjoy a career in computer animation!

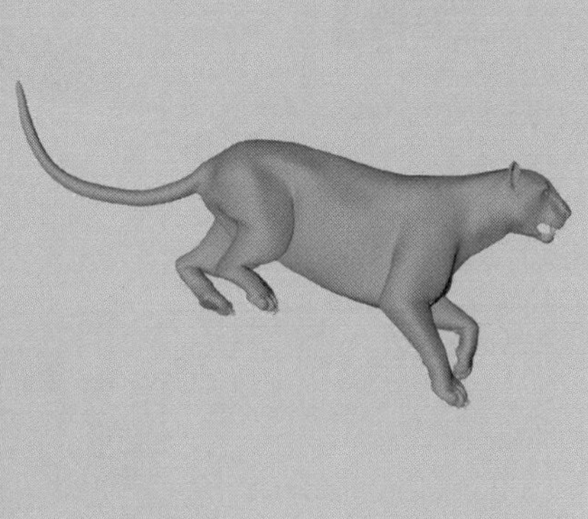

Animators make characters for movies and video games. They use computer programs to design a character and make its body move.

Interactive Glossary

This Interactive Glossary will help you learn how to spell and pronounce a vocabulary term. The Glossary will give you the meaning of the term. It will also show you a picture to help you understand what the term means.

Where you see **Your Turn** write your own words or draw your own picture to help you remember what the term means.

Glossary Pronunciation Key

With every glossary term, there is also a phonetic respelling. A phonetic respelling writes the word the way it sounds. This can help you pronounce new words. Use this key to help you understand the respellings.

Sound	As in	Phonetic Respelling	Sound	As in	Phonetic Respelling
a	bat	(BAT)	oh	over	(OH•ver)
ah	lock	(LAHK)	oo	pool	(POOL)
air	rare	(RAIR)	ow	out	(OWT)
ar	argue	(AR•gyoo)	oy	foil	(FOYL)
aw	law	(LAW)	s	cell	(SEL)
ay	face	(FAYS)		sit	(SIT)
ch	chapel	(CHAP•uhl)	sh	sheep	(SHEEP)
e	test	(TEST)	th	that	(THAT)
	metric	(MEH•trik)		thin	(THIN)
ee	eat	(EET)	u	pull	(PUL)
	feet	(FEET)	uh	medal	(MED•uhl)
	ski	(SKEE)		talent	(TAL•uhnt)
er	paper	(PAY•per)		pencil	(PEN•suhl)
	fern	(FERN)		onion	(UHN•yuhn)
eye	idea	(eye•DEE•uh)		playful	(PLAY•fuhl)
i	bit	(BIT)		dull	(DUHL)
ing	going	(GOH•ing)	y	yes	(YES)
k	card	(KARD)		ripe	(RYP)
	kite	(KYT)	z	bags	(BAGZ)
ngk	bank	(BANGK)	zh	treasure	(TREZH•er)

A

attract [uh·TRAKT]
To pull toward something. (p. 265)

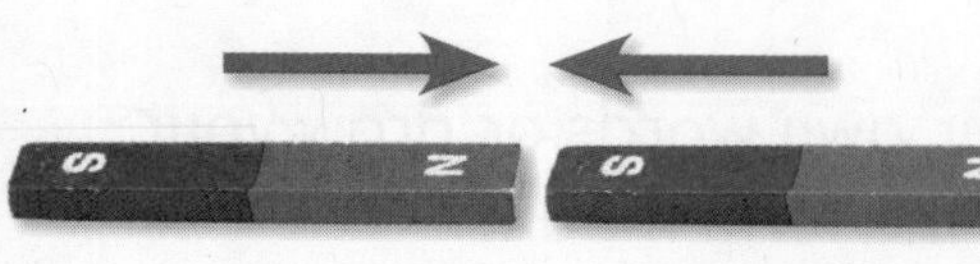

brain [BRAYN]
A part of the body that tells other parts of the body what to do. (p. 288)

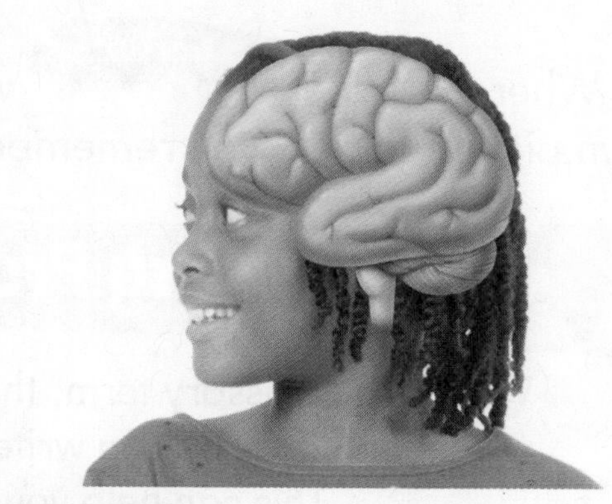

Your Turn

B

basic needs [BAY·sik NEEDZ]
Certain things, such as food, water, air, and shelter, that a living thing needs to survive. (p. 352)

burning [BER·ning]
The changing of a substance into ashes and smoke. (p. 202)

C

clay [KLAY]

Soil that is sticky when wet and smooth when dry. It holds water well, but many kinds of plants don't grow well in it. (p. 103)

communicate [kuh·MYOO·ni·kayt]

To write, draw, or speak to show what you have learned. (p. 31)

Your Turn

condense [kuhn·DENS]

To change from a gas into tiny drops of water. (p. 123)

cone [KOHN]

A part of a pine tree and some other plants where seeds form. (p. 336)

D

design process [dih·ZYN PRAHS·es]

A set of steps that engineers follow to solve problems. (p. 49)

dissolve [di·ZOLV]

To completely mix a solid with a liquid. (p. 200)

draw conclusions [DRAW kuhn·KLOO·zhuhnz]

To use information gathered during an investigation to see whether the results support the hypothesis. (p. 31)

Your Turn

E

electricity [uh·lek·TRIH·sih·tee]

A form of energy. People produce electricity by using energy from other sources. (p. 225)

Your Turn

energy [EN·er·jee]

Something that can cause matter to move or change. (p. 224)

engineer (en·juh·NEER)
A person who uses math and science to design technology that solves problems. (p. 48)

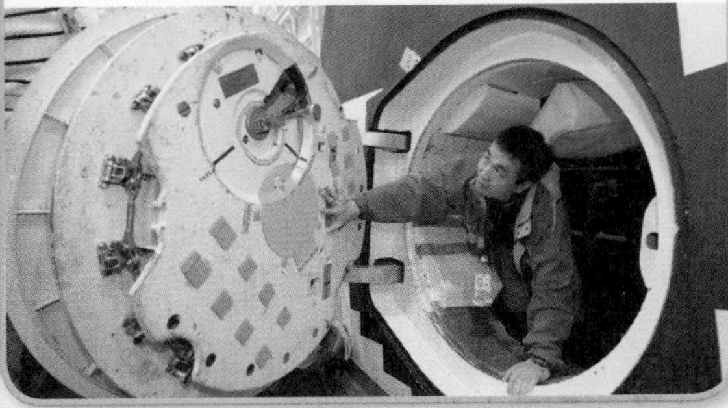

environment [en·VY·ruhn·muhnt]
All the living and nonliving things in a place. (p. 70, 380)

Your Turn

evaporate [ee·VAP·uh·rayt]
To change from a liquid into a gas. (p. 122)

F

force [FAWRS]
A push or a pull. (p. 250)

freeze [FREEZ]

To change from a liquid to a solid. (p. 198)

Your Turn

friction [FRIK·shuhn]

A force that slows or stops things that are touching. Friction also causes objects to get warmer when they rub together. (p. 255)

G

gas [GAS]

A state of matter that fills all the space of its container. (p. 175)

germinate [JER·muh·nayt]

To start to grow. (p. 332)

gills [GILZ]

The parts of some animals that take in oxygen from the water. (p. 363)

gravity [GRAV·ih·tee]
A force that pulls all things toward the center of Earth. (p. 254)

H

habitat [HAB·ih·tat]
The place where a living thing finds food, water, and shelter. (p. 380)

Your Turn

heart [HAHRT]
A muscle that pumps blood throughout the body. (p. 293)

heat [HEET]
A kind of energy that makes things warmer. (p. 225)

humus [HYOO·muhs]
Soil made of once-living things. (p. 103)

hurricane [HER·ih·kayn]
A large storm with heavy rain and strong winds. (p. 139)

hypothesis [hy·PAHTH·uh·sis]
A statement that you can test. (p. 29)

I

inquiry skills [IN·kwer·ee SKILZ]
The skills people use to find out information. (p. 4)

investigate [in·VES·tuh·gayt]
To plan and do a test to answer a question or solve a problem. (p. 28)

Your Turn

life cycle [LYF SY·kuhl]
Changes that happen to an animal or a plant during its life. (p. 313)

L

larva
[LAHR·vuh]
Another name for a caterpillar. (p. 319)

light [LYT]
A kind of energy that lets us see. (p. 225)

lightning [LYT·ning]
A flash of electricity in the sky. (p. 138)

Your Turn

liquid [LIK·wid]
A state of matter that takes the shape of its container. (p. 174)

lungs [LUHNGZ]
The parts of some animals that help them breathe by taking in oxygen from the air. (pp. 292, 362)

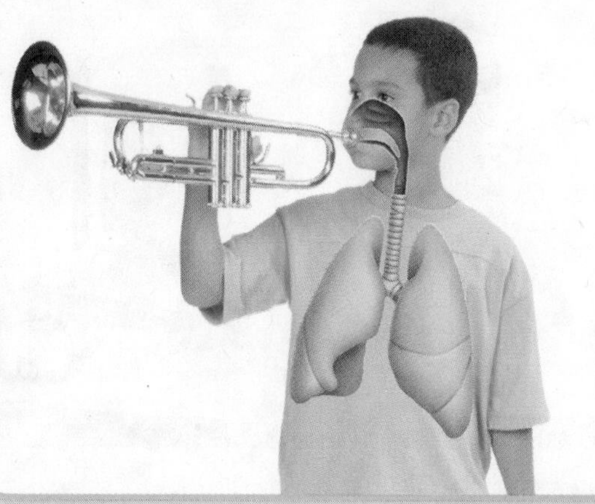

M

magnet [MAG·nit]
An object that can pull things made of iron or steel and can push or pull other magnets. (p. 264)

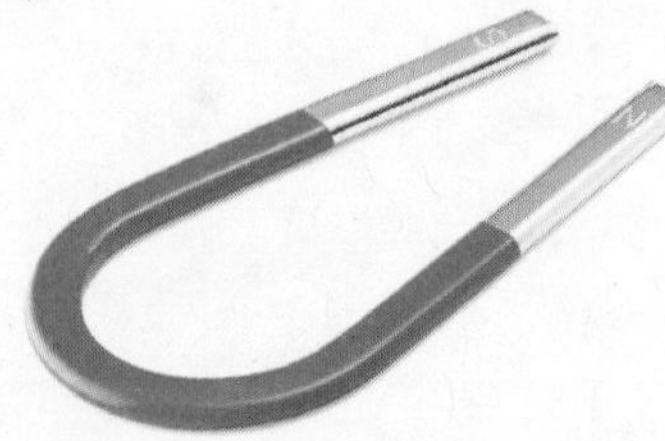

mass [MAS]
The amount of matter in an object. (p. 172)

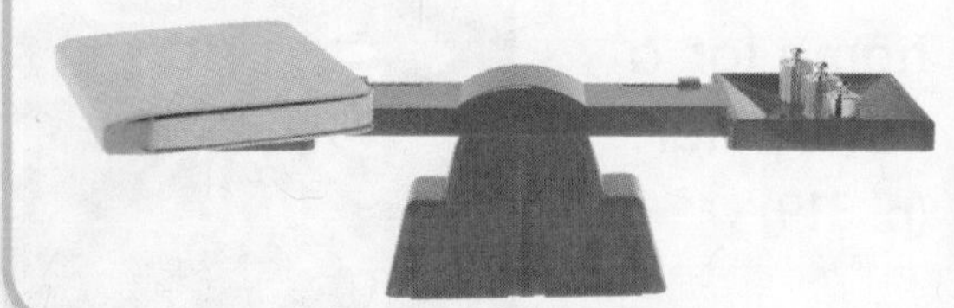

matter [MAT·er]
Anything that takes up space. (p. 158)

Your Turn

measure [MEZH·er]
To find the size, weight, or amount of something. (p. 160)

melt [MELT]
To change from a solid to a liquid. (p. 198)

metamorphosis [met·uh·MAWR·fuh·sis]
A series of changes in appearance that some animals go through. (p. 315)

motion [MOH·shuhn]
When something is moving. Things are in motion when they move. (p. 250)

muscles [MUHS·uhlz]
Body parts that help hold you up and work with bones to help you move. (p. 291)

Your Turn

N

nutrients [NOO·tree·uhnts]
Substances that help plants grow. (p. 355)

P

pole [POHL]
A place on a magnet where the pull is the greatest. (p. 264)

precipitation [pri·sip·uh·TAY·shuhn]
Water that falls from the sky. Rain, snow, sleet, and hail are kinds of precipitation. (p. 120)

property [PRAH·per·tee]
One part of what something is like. Color, size, and shape are each a property. (p. 158)

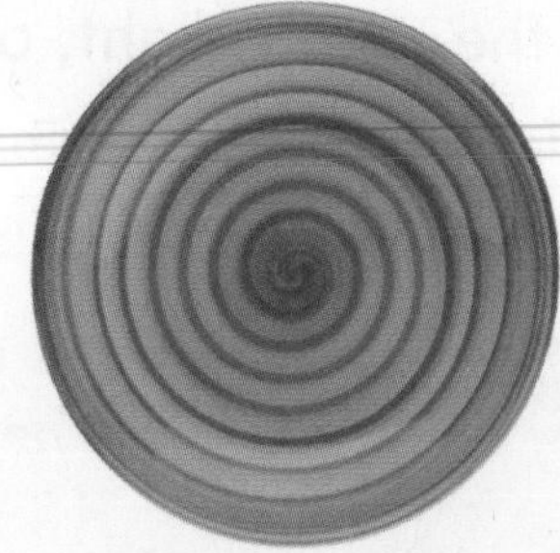

pupa [PYOO·puh]
The part of a life cycle when a caterpillar changes into a butterfly. (p. 319)

R

repel [rih·PEL]
To push away from something. (p. 265)

Your Turn

reproduce [ree·pruh·DOOS]
To have young, or more living things of the same kind. (p. 312)

rock [RAHK]
A hard, nonliving object from the ground. (p. 88)

S

sand [SAND]
Tiny pieces of rock. (p. 103)

seed [SEED]
The part of a plant that new plants grow from. (p. 330)

Your Turn

science tools [SY·uhns TOOLZ]
The tools people use to find out information. (p. 14)

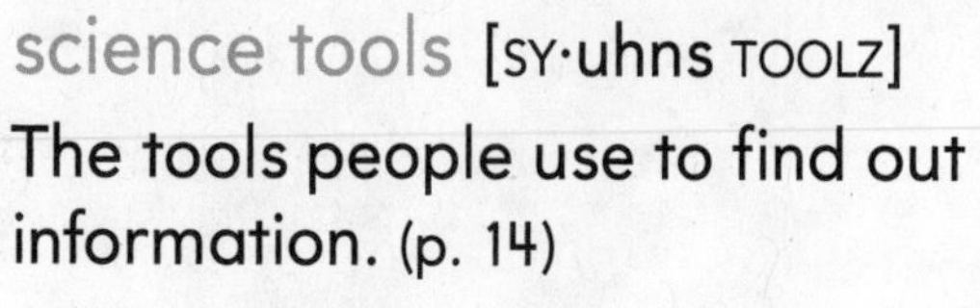

seedling [SEED·ling]
A young plant. (p. 333)

shelter [SHEL·ter]
A safe place to live. (p. 365)

skeleton [SKEL·uh·tuhn]
The bones that support your body and give it shape. (p. 290)

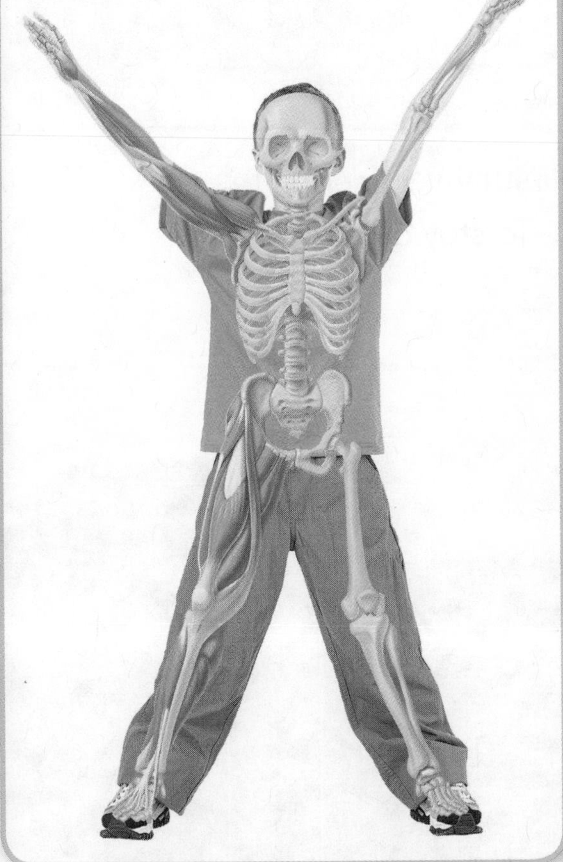

soil [SOYL]
Small pieces of rock and once-living things. (p. 100)

solar energy [SOH·ler EN·er·jee]
Energy from the sun. (p. 225)

solid [SAHL·id]
The only state of matter that has its own shape. (p. 173)

Your Turn

speed [SPEED]
The measure of how fast something moves. (p. 252)

stomach [STUHM·uhk]
A baglike organ in the body that helps digest food. (p. 289)

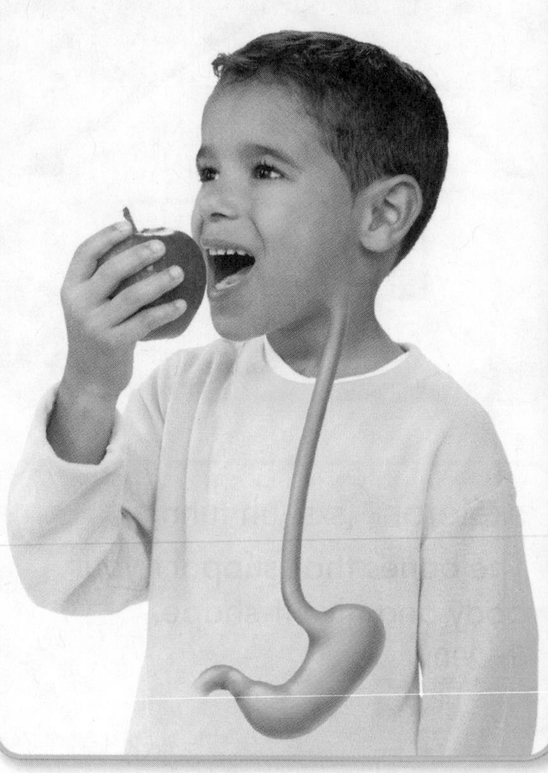

survive [ser·VYV]
To stay alive. (p. 360)

T

tadpole [TAD·pohl]
A young frog that comes out of an egg and has gills to take in oxygen from the water. (p. 314)

technology [tek·NOL·uh·jee]
What engineers make to meet needs and solve problems. (p. 64)

temperature [TEM·per·uh·cher]
A measure of how hot or cold something is. You can measure temperature with a thermometer. (p. 120)

texture [TEKS·cher]
The way something feels. (p. 159)

thermometer [ther·MAHM·uh·ter]
A tool used to measure temperature. (p. 15)

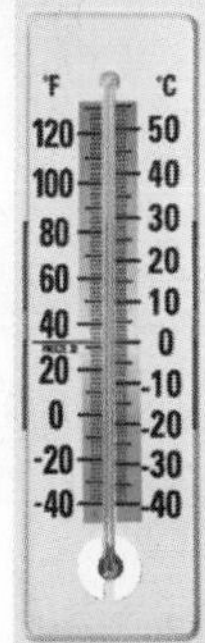

Your Turn

thunderstorm
[THUHN·der·stawrm]
A storm with a lot of rain, thunder, and lightning. (p. 138)

tornado [tawr·NAY·doh]
A spinning cloud with a cone shape. (p. 139)

W

water cycle
[WAW·ter SY·kuhl]
The movement of water from Earth to the air and back again. (p. 122)

Your Turn

water vapor
[WAW·ter VAY·per]
Water in the form of a gas. (p. 176)

weather [WEH·ther]
What the air outside is like.
(p. 118)

weathering [WEH·ther·ing]
A kind of change that happens when wind and water break down rock into smaller pieces.
(p. 89)

Your Turn

weight [WAYT]
A measure of how heavy something feels.
(p. 161)

Index

N

P